Vegetarian Cooking for Good Health

Vegetarian Cooking for Good Health

• • •

Gary Null

and Shelly Null

• • •

COLLIER BOOKS

MACMILLAN PUBLISHING COMPANY
New York

MAXWELL MACMILLAN CANADA
Toronto

MAXWELL MACMILLAN INTERNATIONAL
New York Oxford Singapore Sydney

Collier Books
Macmillan Publishing Company
866 Third Avenue, New York, NY 10022

Collier Macmillan Canada, Inc.
1200 Eglinton Avenue East, Suite 200
Don Mills, Ontario M3C 3N1

Library of Congress Cataloging-in-Publication Data
Null, Gary.
Vegetarian cooking for good health / Gary Null and Shelly Null.
p. cm.
ISBN 0-02-010050-7
1. Vegetarian cookery. I. Null, Shelly. II. Title.
TX837.N85 1991
641.5'636—dc20 91-18102 CIP

Macmillan books are available at special discounts for bulk purchases for sales promotions, premiums, fund-raising, or educational use. For details, contact:

Special Sales Director
Macmillan Publishing Company
866 Third Avenue
New York, NY 10022

10 9 8 7 6 5 4 3 2

Printed in the United States of America

To Alexan and Amber

Acknowledgments

I would like to thank my mother Judy Lutzon, who spent so many days assisting me. She is a special person who made this work a pleasure.

Thanks to my husband Arden for those hours spent in the kitchen, to Andrew Rosenstein for making our time spent at the computer so easy, and to Gerry for his continued support and encouragement during these very special years.

—Shelly Null

Contents

Introduction

We are entering a new period of awareness about not only our health, but about the world. Being healthy has taken on greater importance because we've begun to see how essential our health is to a happy life. We work out at the gym, we go to stress management seminars at the office, we make sure to give time to our family, but sooner or later it's time to eat. Pushing a squeaky-wheeled shopping cart down a supermarket aisle and loading it up with boil-in-a-bag dinners, microwave-in-an-instant meals, or sugary breakfast foods is not the way to total health. Even with our busy schedules it is now entirely possible to prepare delicious, healthy meals quickly! With the success we've had in managing other aspects of our lives, we can now take the time to reestablish our enjoyment of food and cooking. This cookbook will show you the steps you need to take to gradually change the way you eat and move toward a fresher, more wholesome, more exciting cuisine. It's easier than you think and you'll discover that eating right doesn't depend on ingredients you can only find at a health food store three states away.

In light of our concerns about our health, the vegetarian diet will, no doubt, be the diet of choice in the future. The recently released results of a long-term research study on vegetarianism completed by Cornell University and Oxford University, in which a group of 6,500 vegetarians were studied over the course of several years, show that vegetarians have less incidence of cancer, heart disease, and major degenerative diseases like arthritis. In all cases the incidence of these diseases was low to nonexistent. In addition, the study stated that a high-protein diet, which is the typical American diet, was equally as dangerous to the body as a diet high

in fats, something we already know isn't good for us. The study also concluded that vegetarians could receive their daily requirement of calcium from plant sources like spinach and unhulled sesame seeds instead of dairy products, which many vegetarians do not eat. In short, the study lauded vegetarianism and challenged the many nutritional authorities who continue to uphold the belief that one must have a helping each from the "four major food groups" of meat, dairy, grains, and vegetables at each meal. Scientists at Cornell and Oxford have found indisputable evidence that human beings do not nutritionally require meat and dairy products, and, in fact, their consumption is not healthy and can do harm to the body.

Somewhere in the 1920s and '30s we got off track. Around that time, our parents' and grandparents' lives started to change. They may have begun to spend more time at work; with better transportation they could leave home more often. More efficient refrigeration enabled families to choose from a wider range of prepared foods, and diets began to change. The time usually spent preparing and enjoying an at-home meal gave way to other pursuits. With less time available to prepare the meals, families began to rely more on precooked, prepackaged food from manufacturers using newly developed cooking and packaging technology. During the Depression and Dust Bowl years, people began to rely more heavily on cheaper processed food and diner food. The ease and speed with which the early chrome diners, automats, and restaurants could serve its customers were accomplished by serving food that could be prepared ahead of time and kept warm or food that could be prepared fast. Hot dogs, fried chicken, hamburgers, steak, and potatoes all fit the bill. Short-order chefs were quick to realize that anything deep fried took much less time to cook and kept the customer satisfied.

In the 1950s, television held us in its grasp. The family dinner metamorphosized into the TV dinner. Manufacturers capitalized on the demands of people who wanted to eat, but weren't too concerned about what they were eating. A meal on a tray in front of the tube was convenient, and convenience became the culinary goal.

The last thirty years have only seen this situation worsen. Now a meal may be a quick burger and fries or a take-out pizza. The family dinner, in many cases, is a vestige of the old days and saved for special occasions like Thanksgiving. Even then it's easy to buy a precooked turkey, canned cranberries, stuffing mixes, and a prebaked pumpkin pie. Slowly, though, we're beginning to realize that maybe our grandparents knew best. Maybe it was important to take the time to prepare food from scratch. We now know the dangers of a diet consisting of fatty, overprocessed foods, but what can we do about it?

Today, food manufacturers are becoming increasingly aware of the changes many of us want to make in our diets and are producing all sorts of products that are reduced in fat, calories, and sugar. However, these "lite" foods, as the industry sometimes calls them, may be highly processed, and some contain artificial sweeteners that may be carcinogins, which can cause sudden mood alterations. While these processed, calorie-reduced foods may be slightly better in some ways than their alternatives, they are not the way to a healthier life. It takes more than that. Some of the foods found in the average home's refrigerator may be so loaded with preservatives, sugar, or salt that they actually have an indefinite shelf life. The first step in beginning a change in your eating habits is to realize that any food that doesn't go bad *is* bad for you.

Alterations in your diet don't have to be difficult; just the desire to change will help, though these modifications do need to be coupled with other life-impacting changes. If you've suddenly come to the realization that the food you've eaten all your life is not healthy, how do you really begin a healthy overhaul?

You can use this cookbook as a guide to help you make positive changes in all aspects of your life. If you feel that you don't have full control of your life, are overeating or eating the wrong things, or are unhappy with yourself, then you should take a close look at what you want to change in your life to enhance your health. Since strategy is important when making changes, set realistic goals for yourself and design your own program to meet these goals.

This is more than a cookbook: it's a way to re-empower yourself and take control. Science has found that food plays a bigger part in our health than we had previously realized, and a diet rich in grains, a variety of fresh vegetables, and an occasional small serving of fish can all work together to keep us in optimal health. The recipes that follow are designed to do just that—to promote wellness. Some of the recipes are designed for people with food allergies or an interest in their cholesterol levels and losing weight, suggesting alternatives to problematic foods like milk and eggs. If you are not ready to eliminate those foods from your diet, or if you are a long time "meat and potatoes" eater, use the recipes in this cookbook to help you make a smooth transition to vegetarianism.

Using this cookbook, you can turn things around and begin to enjoy wholesome, simpler foods with easy-to-find ingredients and easy preparation methods, and return to the time when a meal offered us an opportunity to enjoy delicious, healthy foods. It doesn't have to take as long as it took your grandmother because we now have modern appliances. Use the recipes here as a basis for starting your own healthy traditions and enhancing your health. Each recipe in this book has been thoroughly tested by hundreds of people for taste and ease of preparation. Give this book a chance and you can start making healthy changes right now.

CHAPTER 1

Breakfast

Banana-Coconut Buckwheat Cereal

1/3	*cup uncooked cream of buckwheat*
2 3/4	*cups water*
1/2	*cup mashed banana*
1/4	*cup coconut flakes*
3	*tablespoons raisins*
1/4	*cup wheat germ (optional)*
2	*to 3 tablespoons pure maple syrup*
1 1/2	*teaspoons ground cinnamon*

Combine the buckwheat and water in a medium-size saucepan and bring to a boil over medium heat. Cook 3 to 7 minutes, then add the remaining ingredients and cook another 1 to 2 minutes. Serve with soy milk or piña colada juice on top.

YIELD: 2 SERVINGS

Carob Rice Cereal

1/3	*cup uncooked cream of brown rice*
2 1/2	*cups water*
1/4	*cup sunflower seeds*
1/4	*cup sesame seeds*
1/4	*cup pumpkin seeds*
2	*teaspoons vanilla extract*
1/4	*cup chopped dates*
1	*tablespoon carob powder*
1/4	*cup pure maple syrup*
1	*tablespoon ground cinnamon*

Combine the rice and water in a medium-size saucepan and bring to boil over medium heat. Reduce the heat to low, add the remaining ingredients, and cook 5 to 7 minutes. Serve hot with pear nectar or apple juice on top.

YIELD: 2 SERVINGS

Hawaiian Rice Cereal

1½ *cups coconut milk or tropical fruit juice*
1 *banana, sliced*
½ *cup pitted fresh or frozen cherries*
½ *cup chopped pineapple*
¼ *cup shredded unsweetened coconut*
2 *cups cooked white basmati rice*
½ *cup chopped macadamia nuts, toasted (see note below)*

In a medium-size saucepan, combine the milk, banana, cherries, and pineapple. Cook over medium-low heat for 2 to 3 minutes. Add the remaining ingredients, mix well, and cook an additional 2 to 3 minutes. Serve hot.

YIELD: 2 SERVINGS

Note: To toast nuts, preheat oven to 375° and place nuts on an ungreased cookie sheet for 10 to 15 minutes or until light brown.

Peachy Bulgur

1 1/4 cups soy milk
2 tablespoons currants or raisins
1 cup sliced peaches
2 cups cooked bulgur
1 teaspoon vanilla or orange extract
1/8 teaspoon ground cinnamon or nutmeg
1/4 cup whole almonds

In a medium-size saucepan, combine the milk, currants, and peaches. Cook over low heat for 1 to 2 minutes. Add the remaining ingredients and cook for an additional 1 to 2 minutes. Mix well and serve hot or cold.

YIELD: 2 SERVINGS

Blueberry-Apricot Oatmeal

3/4 cup rolled oats
1 cup water
1/2 cup apricot nectar or apple-apricot juice
1/2 banana, sliced
1/2 cup fresh or frozen blueberries
1 1/2 to 2 tablespoons pure maple syrup (optional)

Combine all the ingredients in a medium-size saucepan and cook for 8 to 10 minutes or until done over medium heat.

YIELD: 2 SERVINGS

Carob-Blueberry Cream of Wheat

- 2 *cups cooked farina*
- 2 *tablespoons carob powder*
- ½ *cup chopped Brazil nuts*
- 1 *cup fresh or frozen blueberries*
- ¼ *cup pure maple syrup*
- 1 *teaspoon ground nutmeg*

Combine all the ingredients in a medium-size saucepan and mix well. Cook over low heat for 2 to 3 minutes, stir, and serve hot.

YIELD: 2 SERVINGS

Creamy Carob-Coconut Millet

- 1¼ *cups coconut milk*
- 2 *tablespoons raisins*
- ½ *teaspoon vanilla extract*
- 3 *cups cooked millet*
- 2 *tablespoons carob powder*
- 2 *tablespoons chopped walnuts*
- 2 *tablespoons sunflower seeds*
- ¼ *cup sliced bananas*
- ½ *teaspoon ground nutmeg*
- ¼ *cup toasted shredded coconut*

Combine the milk, raisins, and vanilla in a medium-size saucepan. Bring to a simmer over low heat. Add the remaining ingredients, stir well, cook an additional 1 to 2 minutes, and serve either hot or cold.

YIELD: 2 SERVINGS

Apple-Cinnamon French Toast with Banana Sauce

- ½ *cup applesauce*
- 1 *cup soy milk*
- 1 *teaspoon ground cinnamon*
- 1 *teaspoon vanilla extract*
- 2 *large eggs*
- 3 *tablespoons sunflower or safflower oil*
- 4 *slices bread of your choice*
- 3 *bananas, pureed*
- ⅓ *cup pure maple syrup*
- ¼ *cup chopped nuts of your choice*

Combine the applesauce, milk, cinnamon, vanilla, and eggs in a medium-size bowl and mix with a whisk or fork. Heat the oil in a skillet over medium heat. Soak the bread on both sides in the mixture, then fry till light brown on both sides. Serve hot, topped with the banana puree, syrup, and nuts.

YIELD: 2 SERVINGS

Blueberry-Banana Pancakes

½ *cup whole wheat flour*
¼ *cup wheat germ*
1 *teaspoon baking powder*
1 *teaspoon baking soda*
Dash of ground nutmeg
1 *cup plain yogurt*
½ *cup thinly sliced bananas*
¾ *cup fresh or frozen blueberries*
¼ *cup oil (sunflower, soy, or safflower)*

In a medium-size mixing bowl, combine the flour, wheat germ, baking powder, baking soda, and nutmeg. Mix well with a fork to remove lumps. Mix in the yogurt, bananas, and blueberries. Heat the oil in a large skillet over medium heat. Pour 3 to 4 tablespoons of batter into the oil at a time and cook for 2 to 3 minutes on each side until light brown.

YIELD: 12 PANCAKES

Buckwheat-Banana Pancakes

- 1 *cup plain yogurt*
- 1 *large egg*
- 1 *teaspoon vanilla extract*
- 1 *banana, mashed*
- 1/4 *cup soy milk*
- 1/4 *cup toasted wheat germ*
- 1/4 *cup whole wheat flour*
- 1/2 *cup buckwheat flour*
- 1 *teaspoon baking powder*
- 1 *teaspoon baking soda*
- 2 *tablespoons raisins*
- 3 *tablespoons shredded unsweetened coconut (optional)*
- 3 *tablespoons oil (sunflower, soy, or safflower)*

In a medium-size mixing bowl, combine the yogurt, egg, vanilla, banana, and milk, mixing with a fork until well blended. In a separate bowl, combine the wheat germ, flours, baking powder, and baking soda, mixing well. Add the flour mixture to the yogurt mixture, blending well with a spoon. Stir in the raisins and coconut. Heat the oil in a large skillet over medium heat. Pour in 2 to 3 tablespoons of batter at a time and cook for 3 to 5 minutes on each side until light brown.

YIELD: 12 PANCAKES

Cinnamon-Pear Pancakes

- ½ *cup peeled, sliced pear, steamed 5 minutes*
- ¼ *cup soy milk*
- 1 *medium egg*
- 2 *tablespoons pure maple syrup*
- 1 *teaspoon ground cinnamon*
- ½ *teaspoon ground nutmeg*
- 1 *teaspoon vanilla or almond extract*
- 1½ *teaspoons baking powder*
- ½ *cup barley flour*
- 3 *tablespoons safflower oil*

Blend all the ingredients, except the oil, in a medium-size mixing bowl with a fork or whisk until smooth. Heat the oil in a large skillet over medium heat. Add 3 tablespoons of batter at a time and cook the pancake on one side for 4 minutes or until done. Flip over and cook for an additional 3 minutes. Serve with maple syrup.

YIELD: ABOUT 8 PANCAKES

Tasty Buckwheat Pancakes

2 3/4 *cups buckwheat flour*
2 *large eggs*
1 1/2 *teaspoons baking powder*
1 *teaspoon carob powder*
1 1/2 *teaspoons ground cinnamon*
1 *cup soy milk*
1/4 *cup raisins*
1/4 *cup chopped pecans or cashews*
1 *large banana, mashed*
3 *tablespoons pure maple syrup*
2 *teaspoons vanilla extract*
3/4 *cup water*
1 *teaspoon canola oil or safflower oil*

Blend all the ingredients, except the oil, in a medium-size mixing bowl with a fork or whisk until smooth. Heat the oil in a skillet over medium heat. Add three tablespoons of batter at a time and cook the pancake on one side for 4 minutes or until done. Flip over and cook for an additional 3 minutes. Serve with maple syrup.

YIELD: ABOUT 15 PANCAKES

Mozzarella-Walnut Omelet

- 3 *large eggs*
- ½ *teaspoon salt*
- ¼ *teaspoon freshly ground black pepper*
- 4½ *teaspoons extra virgin olive oil*
- ¼ *cup chopped walnuts*
- 1 *cup grated mozzarella cheese*
- ¾ *cup chopped fresh tomatoes*
- 2 *tablespoons minced fresh basil*

Whisk together the eggs, ¼ teaspoon of the salt, and ⅛ teaspoon of the pepper. Heat the oil in a large saucepan over medium heat, then pour in the egg mixture and cook, covered, for 3 to 4 minutes. Sprinkle the walnuts and cheese on top, cover, and cook an additional 2 to 3 minutes. Fold one half of the omelet onto the other and place on a plate. Serve with the tomatoes, basil, and remaining salt and pepper on top.

YIELD: 2 SERVINGS

Pesto-Tomato Omelet

- 3 *large eggs*
- ¼ *cup Pesto (see page 196)*
- 1 *teaspoon butter or extra virgin olive oil*
- ½ *cup chopped fresh tomatoes*
- ⅛ *to ¼ teaspoon freshly ground black pepper*

Whisk together the eggs and Pesto in a medium-size bowl. Heat the butter over medium heat in a large saucepan, pour in the egg mixture, cover, and cook for 4 to 5 minutes. Sprinkle the tomatoes and pepper on top, cover, and cook an additional 1 to 2 minutes. Fold half of the omelet onto the other half and serve.

YIELD: 1 SERVING

Orange Marmalade

- 1 ½ *teaspoons grated orange rind*
- ¾ *cup orange juice*
- 2 *tablespoons pure maple syrup*
- 2 *tablespoons honey*

Combine all the ingredients in a medium-size saucepan and cook for 5 to 10 minutes over medium heat. Remove from heat and pour into a small bowl. Chill for 2 to 3 hours. Will keep for two weeks if refrigerated.

YIELD: 1 CUP

CHAPTER 2

Drinks

Frozen Cherry Supreme

- 3 *cups orange juice*
- 1 *cup ice cubes*
- ½ *cup frozen cherries*
- 1 *banana*
- ¼ *teaspoon ground cinnamon*

Combine all the ingredients in a blender and blend until smooth.

YIELD: 2 SERVINGS

Papaya-Orange Surprise

- 1 *cup soy milk*
- ½ *cup sliced papaya*
- 1 *cup orange juice*
- 1 *banana*
- ½ *teaspoon ground cinnamon*
- 1 *cup ice cubes*

Combine all the ingredients in a blender and blend until smooth.

YIELD: 2 SERVINGS

Nectarine-Papaya Shake

- 1 *cup chopped papaya*
- 3 *to 4 tablespoons fresh lime juice*
- 1 *cup ice cubes*
- 1 *cup piña colada juice*
- 3/4 *cup sliced nectarine*

Combine all the ingredients in a blender and blend until smooth.

YIELD: 2 SERVINGS

Papaya-Pineapple Shake

- 2 *cups soy milk*
- 1/2 *cup chopped papaya*
- 1 *banana*
- 1/4 *cup drained pineapple chunks*
- 1/2 *teaspoon lemon extract*
- 1 *cup ice cubes*

Combine all the ingredients in a blender and blend until smooth.

YIELD: 2 SERVINGS

Power Boom Shake

1 ¼ cups apple juice
1 ¼ cups pear nectar
1 ½ cups water
1 ½ to 2 bananas
4 tablespoons Nu-Trim Protein Powder or any type of protein powder
3 tablespoons maple vanilla powder (optional; available in health food stores)
1 ½ teaspoons carob powder
½ cup ice cubes

Combine all the ingredients in a blender and blend until smooth.

YIELD: 2 SERVINGS

Very Berry Shake

- 1 *cup fresh or frozen blueberries, strawberries, or blackberries*
- 1 1/4 *cups soy milk*
- 1 *banana*
- 3 *tablespoons pure maple syrup*
- 1 *cup ice cubes*

Combine all the ingredients in a blender and blend until smooth.

YIELD: 2 SERVINGS

Banana Shake

- 2 *cups soy milk*
- 2 *bananas*
- 1/4 *teaspoon vanilla extract*
- 1/4 *teaspoon ground nutmeg*
- 3 *tablespoons pure maple syrup (optional)*
- 1 *cup ice cubes*

Combine all the ingredients in a blender and blend until smooth.

YIELD: 2 SERVINGS

Caroby Pear Shake

- 3 *cups soy milk*
- ½ *cup pear juice*
- 2 *cups sesame seeds*
- 2 *tablespoons wheat germ*
- 1 *tablespoon carob powder*
- ½ *teaspoon ground cinnamon*
- 2 *cups ice cubes*
- 1 *banana*

Combine all the ingredients in a blender and blend until smooth.

YIELD: 2 SERVINGS

Hot Carob Drink

- 4 *cups soy milk*
- ¼ *cup date sugar or pure maple syrup*
- ½ *cup carob powder*
- 2 *teaspoons vanilla extract*

Combine all the ingredients in a medium-size saucepan and simmer over medium heat for 2 to 3 minutes. Serve hot in mugs.

YIELD: 2 SERVINGS

CHAPTER 3

Appetizers

Grandma Null's Stuffed Eggs

- 2 *large hard-boiled eggs, halved*
- ½ *teaspoon chopped fresh parsley*
- 2 *tablespoons mayonnaise*
- ¼ *teaspoon apple cider vinegar*
- ½ *teaspoon prepared mustard*
- ¼ *teaspoon salt*
- ⅛ *teaspoon freshly ground black pepper*
- *Paprika for garnish*

Remove the yolks from the eggs. Place in a mixing bowl. Add the parsley, mayonnaise, vinegar, and mustard and mix with a fork until creamy. Add the salt and pepper and mix again. Stuff the mixture back into the eggs and garnish with paprika.

YIELD: 4 STUFFED HALVES

Holiday Stuffed Mushrooms

- 24 *large mushroom caps*
- 1 ½ *cups chopped mushroom stems*
- ½ *cup extra virgin olive oil*
- 1 *ripe avocado, mashed*
- ¾ *cup fine bread crumbs*
- ⅓ *cup chopped fresh parsley*
- 1 *teaspoon salt*
- ¼ *teaspoon freshly ground black pepper*
- ½ *teaspoon dried sage*
- ½ *teaspoon dried rosemary*
- ½ *teaspoon dried thyme*

Place the mushroom caps into a baking dish. Combine the remaining ingredients in a large bowl, mix well, then place the mixture by the teaspoonful into the caps. Bake in a preheated 400°F oven for 25 to 35 minutes.

YIELD: 24 STUFFED CAPS

Sweetly Stuffed Tiny Red Peppers

- 2 *tablespoons chopped pecans*
- 2 *tablespoons chopped dates*
- 1/4 *cup apple butter*
- 1/2 *teaspoon ground cinnamon*
- 1/2 *cup diced mushrooms*
- 4 *tiny red peppers, cored and seeded*

Combine all the ingredients, except the peppers, in a medium-size bowl and mix well. Stuff the mixture into the peppers. Place the peppers in a small baking dish, cover with aluminum foil, and bake in a preheated 375°F oven for 35 minutes.

YIELD: 2 SERVINGS

Potato Boats Stuffed with Adzuki Beans and Cheese

- 3 *Idaho potatoes, baked, halved, with center taken out and skins set aside*
- 1 *tablespoon chopped fresh rosemary*
- 2 *tablespoons chopped fresh parsley*
- 1 *cup mashed adzuki beans*
- ½ *teaspoon paprika*
- ½ *teaspoon salt*
- ½ *teaspoon freshly ground black pepper*
- 1 *cup shredded cheddar cheese (optional)*
- 2 *to 3 tablespoons extra virgin olive oil*

In a large bowl, combine all the ingredients in the order in which they are listed. Stuff the mixture back into the skins and bake in a preheated 425°F for 10 minutes.

YIELD: 2 SERVINGS

Broiled Vegetables with an Herb Vinaigrette Dressing

- 2 *leeks, quartered*
- 2 *red bell peppers, quartered*
- 2 *yellow zucchini, halved*

DRESSING

2 *teaspoons chopped fresh chives*
1 *tablespoon chopped fresh parsley*
½ *cup apple cider vinegar*
2 *teaspoons prepared mustard*
1 *cup extra virgin olive oil*
1 *tablespoon fresh lemon juice*
1 *teaspoon salt*
½ *teaspoon freshly ground black pepper*
½ *cup water*

Place the vegetables under a preheated broiler for about 3 to 5 minutes; be careful not to burn. Arrange on a plate. Combine the dressing ingredients and pour over the vegetables. The vegetables can also be grilled, if desired.

YIELD: 2 SERVINGS

Italian Eggplant Terrine

3 *to 5 cups water*
1 *cup peeled, sliced eggplant*
1 *tablespoon salt*
2 *tablespoons extra virgin olive oil*
1 *cup goat cheese*
1 *cup roasted peppers (2 jars, prepared)*
½ *cup chopped fresh basil*

In a large mixing bowl, combine the water, eggplant, and salt, and let soak for 2 hours. Lightly oil 4 small terrines (1 cup). Place a layer of eggplant in the bottom of each terrine, then a layer of cheese, followed by a layer of peppers, a layer of basil, another layer of cheese, then the remainder of the eggplant. Cover each terrine with aluminum foil, then place in a pan of water so the water comes half way up on the outside of the terrine. Bake in a preheated 375°F oven for 30 minutes.

YIELD: FOUR 1-CUP TERRINES

Cold Eggplant Spread

- 1 *small eggplant*
- 1 *tablespoon chopped fresh tomatoes*
- 1/4 *teaspoon crushed garlic*
- 1/2 *teaspoon extra virgin olive oil*
- 1/4 *teaspoon fresh lemon juice*
- 1 *tablespoon chopped fresh parsley*
- 1 *tablespoon diced onions*
- 1/8 *teaspoon salt*

Broil eggplant in oven for 15 to 25 minutes until it pops open. Remove the center with a spoon, discard the skin, then run through a food processor or blender until mushy, or use a fork. Add the remaining ingredients, mix well, and chill for 1 to 2 hours. Great with chips or crackers.

YIELD: 3/4 CUP

Sweet Nutty Spread

- ¼ *cup tahini*
- ½ *cup honey*
- 2 *tablespoons chopped almonds*
- 2 *tablespoons chopped Brazil nuts*

Combine all the ingredients in a medium-size mixing bowl and mix well. Great on sandwiches, crackers, or rice crackers! It will store in the refrigerator for two to three weeks.

YIELD: ABOUT 1 CUP

Spicy Guacamole

- 1 *cup ripe avocado*
- 1 *tablespoon fresh lemon juice*
- 2 *teaspoons diced red onions*
- 2 *teaspoons chopped fresh parsley*
- ⅛ *teaspoon cayenne pepper*
- 1 *teaspoon salt*
- *Dash of freshly ground black pepper*

Combine all the ingredients in medium-size bowl, mix well with a fork, and chill for 1 hour. Serve with tortilla chips.

YIELD: 1½ CUPS

Easy Avocado Dip

- 1 *cup chopped ripe avocado*
- 2 *tablespoons fresh lemon juice*
- ¼ *cup chopped fresh tomatoes*
- 2 *tablespoons chopped onions*
- 1 *teaspoon crushed garlic*
- 2 *teaspoons prepared mustard*
- 2 *teaspoons chopped fresh dill*

Combine all the ingredients in a blender or food processor and process until smooth. Serve at room temperature with tortilla chips, possibly blue corn.

YIELD: 1½ CUPS

Creamy Tofu Dip

- 2 *cups silken tofu*
- 2 *tablespoons chopped fresh parsley*
- 2 *tablespoons prepared mustard*
- ½ *cup mayonnaise*
- 2 *tablespoons apple cider vinegar*
- 1 *teaspoon salt*
- ½ *teaspoon freshly ground black pepper*
- 2 *tablespoons chopped fresh dill*
- *Paprika for garnish*

Process all the ingredients, except the paprika, in a food processor or blender until smooth. Sprinkle with paprika. Serve chilled with raw carrot and celery sticks and broccoli and cauliflower florets.

YIELD: 2½ TO 3 CUPS

Tahini-Broccoli Cream Dip

- 1 *cup silken tofu*
- ½ *cup tahini*
- 2 *tablespoons tamari*
- ½ *cup chopped broccoli, steamed 2 to 4 minutes*
- 1 *tablespoon chopped scallions*
- ¼ *teaspoon freshly ground black pepper*

Combine all the ingredients in a blender or food processor and process until smooth. Serve cold.

YIELD: 2 TO 4 SERVINGS (2 CUPS)

QUICK CARROT DIP: Substitute steamed chopped carrots for the broccoli and sliced fresh chives for the scallions.

Party Bean Dip

½ cup canned chickpeas
¼ cup tahini
2 tablespoons chopped fresh parsley
½ teaspoon salt
¼ teaspoon freshly ground black pepper
¼ cup silken tofu
4½ teaspoons fresh lemon juice

Combine all the ingredients in a blender or food processor until smooth. Serve with pita bread, carrot sticks, or bread sticks.

YIELD: ABOUT 1¼ CUPS

Zesty Black Bean Dip

2 cups canned black beans
½ cup chopped fresh tomatoes
1 cup sour cream or yogurt
6 tablespoons chopped onions
2 tablespoons chopped fresh chives
2 teaspoons salt
½ teaspoon freshly ground black pepper
1 teaspoon paprika

Combine all the ingredients, except the paprika, briefly in a food processor or blender. Chill for 1 to 2 hours, then garnish with the paprika. Serve with blue or yellow tortilla chips.

YIELD: ABOUT 4 CUPS

Spicy Tomato Salsa

- 1 *cup chopped fresh tomatoes*
- 1/8 *to 1/4 cup chopped onions*
- 1 *tablespoon chopped fresh parsley*
- 3 *to 4 tablespoons chopped fresh basil*
- 1 *teaspoon salt*
- 1/2 *teaspoon freshly ground black pepper*
- 1 *tablespoon extra virgin olive oil (optional)*
- 2 *tablespoons minced fresh hot peppers (optional)*

Combine all the ingredients in a medium-size bowl until well mixed. Chill 1 to 2 hours before serving with chips. It will keep in the refrigerator for two days, but stir before serving.

YIELD: ABOUT 1½ CUPS

Sourdough Rye Crackers

1½ cups plus 2 tablespoons rye flour
½ cup water
1 package sourdough starter
½ teaspoon salt
1 teaspoon baking powder
3 tablespoons safflower oil

Combine 2 tablespoons of the rye flour, the water, and the sourdough starter. Let stand, covered, at 75°F for 36 hours. Add the remaining flour, the salt, baking powder, and oil, and mix well with your hands. Form into a ball and roll out on a floured counter with a rolling pin or press to ⅛- to ¼-inch thickness with the palm of your hand. Press with a biscuit mold or cut into appropriate cracker size (about 2 inches). Bake on a greased cookie sheetinapreheated375°F oven for 25 minutes or until light brown.

YIELD: 12 CRACKERS

Oat Pine Nut Crackers

3 tablespoons safflower oil
1 tablespoon egg substitute
½ cup plus 1 tablespoon amazake (almond)
2 tablespoons pine nuts
¼ teaspoon salt
1 cup oat flour

Combine all the ingredients in a medium-size bowl and mix well with your hands. Roll the dough into a ball, then, using a rolling pin, roll the dough onto a floured surface until it is 1/8- to 1/4-inch thick. Press out with cookie cutters or cut into 2-inch crackers with a knife. Bake on a greased cookie sheet in a preheated 375°F for 25 minutes or until very lightly browned.

YIELD: 12 TO 16 CRACKERS

VARIATIONS: ***Rye Crackers:*** Use sunflower oil instead of safflower oil and caraway seeds instead of pine nuts. ***Rye Cheese Sticks:*** After combining all the ingredients for rye crackers, add 1 cup grated cheddar cheese and another 1/4 cup caraway or sesame seeds. Roll the dough into a ball, then take small pieces of dough the size of half dollars and roll between the palms of your hands until they're pencil-shaped. Bake on a greased cookie sheet in a preheated 350°F oven for 20 minutes. Makes 24 sticks.

CHAPTER 4

Soups

Onion Soup

- 4 *cups sliced yellow onions*
- ¼ *cup chopped fresh parsley*
- ¼ *cup extra virgin olive oil*
- 2 *vegetable bouillon cubes (Morga)*
- ½ *teaspoon freshly ground black pepper*
- 2¼ *teaspoons dried basil*
- 1½ *teaspoons garlic powder*
- 3 *to 4 cups water (depending on the consistency you like)*

In a large pot, sauté the onions and parsley in the oil over medium-high heat until the onions are clear. Add the remaining ingredients, reduce the heat to medium, and cook, covered, for 20 minutes.

YIELD: 2 TO 3 SERVINGS

Vitamin-fortified Vegetable Soup

- 1/4 *cup chopped red onions*
- 1/2 *cup sliced leeks*
- 1 *scallion, sliced*
- 1/8 *teaspoon salt*
- 1/8 *teaspoon freshly ground black pepper*
- 1 *clove garlic, pressed*
- 1 1/2 *teaspoons extra virgin olive oil*
- 4 *to 6 cups water (depending on the consistency you like)*
- 1 *celery stalk, sliced*
- 1/2 *cup sliced yellow squash*
- 1/2 *cup sliced turnips*
- 1/2 *cup sliced carrots*
- 1/4 *cup sliced parsnips*
- 1/4 *cup chopped snow peas*
- 3/4 *cup chopped green cabbage*
- 1 *cup prepared tomato sauce*
- 2 *tablespoons Spike or 1 vegetable bouillon cube (Morga)*
- 1 *teaspoon salt*
- 1 *teaspoon freshly ground black pepper*
- 1 *teaspoon paprika*
- 1 *teaspoon garlic powder*
- 2 *tablespoons chopped fresh parsley*
- 1 *tablespoon chopped fresh dill*
- 1 *teaspoon dried savory or marjoram*
- 1 *teaspoon dried oregano*

In a large saucepan, sauté the onions, leeks, scallions, salt, pepper, and garlic in the oil over medium-high heat for 2 to 3 minutes. Add the remaining ingredients, bring to a boil, and reduce the heat to medium to low. Cover and cook for 45 to 50 minutes.

YIELD: 3 SERVINGS

Hearty Winter Soup

- 1/4 *cup chopped onions*
- 3/4 *cup sliced carrots*
- 3/4 *cup sliced leeks*
- 1 *tablespoon extra virgin olive oil*
- 3 *to 4 cups water (depending on the consistency you like)*
- 1 *teaspoon tamari*
- 1/2 *cup dried red lentils, soaked overnight in water and drained*
- 1/4 *cup pink beans, canned (optional)*
- 1/2 *cup chopped butternut squash*
- 1/4 *teaspoon celery seed*
- 1/2 *teaspoon salt*
- 1/8 *teaspoon freshly ground black pepper*
- 1/2 *teaspoon cumin seed*
- 1/4 *teaspoon curry powder*
- 1 *vegetable bouillon cube (Morga)*

In a large saucepan, sauté the onions, carrots, and leeks in the oil over medium-high heat for 5 minutes. Add the remaining ingredients, cover, and cook for 45 to 60 minutes over medium heat. Serve with rice and a salad.

YIELD: 2 TO 3 SERVINGS

Exceptional Noodle Soup

- 3 *tablespoons extra virgin olive oil*
- ½ *cup sliced zucchini*
- ½ *cup sliced carrots*
- ½ *cup sliced potatoes*
- ½ *cup sliced celery*
- ¼ *cup diced onions*
- ¼ *cup sliced mushrooms*
- ¼ *cup chopped fresh parsley*
- ½ *cup cauliflower florets*
- 1 *teaspoon salt*
- ¼ *teaspoon freshly ground black pepper*
- 1 *vegetable bouillon cube (Morga)*
- 2 *bay leaves*
- ¼ *cup chopped fresh dill*
- 6 *cups water*
- 2 *cups uncooked egg noodles*

In a large saucepan, heat the oil over medium heat and sauté the vegetables about 10 minutes. Add the remaining ingredients, except the noodles, and let simmer over medium-low heat 25 to 35 minutes. Add the noodles 10 minutes before finishing.

YIELD: 4 SERVINGS

Sabzi Ka Shorba (Fresh-mixed Vegetable Soup)

- 1¾ *to 3 cups water (depending on the consistency you like)*
- 1 *cup dried yellow lentils*
- 1½ *cups sliced carrots*
- 1½ *cups cauliflower florets*
- 1½ *cups broccoli florets*
- ½ *teaspoon ground cumin*
- ¼ *teaspoon chat masala*
- 1 *tablespoon chopped fresh cilantro*
- ½ *teaspoon salt*

Combine all the ingredients in a large saucepan and cook 25 to 35 minutes over medium heat.

YIELD: 2 SERVINGS

Mushroom Barley Soup

- 2 *cups sliced mushrooms*
- 1 *cup sliced leeks*
- ½ *cup diced carrots*
- ½ *cup diced onions*
- 2 *tablespoons extra virgin olive oil*
- ¾ *cup cooked barley*
- 2½ *cups water*
- 3 *tablespoons chopped fresh dill*
- 2¼ *teaspoons sea salt*
- ½ *teaspoon freshly ground black pepper*

In a large saucepan, sauté the mushrooms, leeks, carrots, and onions in the oil for 3 to 5 minutes over medium-high heat. Add the remaining ingredients and cook, covered, over medium to low heat for 35 to 45 minutes.

YIELD: 3 SERVINGS

Chinese Mushroom Soup

- ½ *cup chopped leeks*
- 1 *scallion, chopped*
- 1 *tablespoon sesame oil*
- ¼ *teaspoon hot sesame oil*
- 1 *tablespoon tamari*

2 *cloves garlic, sliced*
1½ *teaspoons freshly grated ginger*
½ *cup diced firm tofu*
½ *cup miso paste*
5 *cups water*
½ *cup water chestnuts (measured then chopped)*
½ *cup bamboo shoots (measured then chopped)*
¼ *cup dried black mushrooms*
¼ *cup tree ear mushrooms*
½ *cup shiitake mushrooms (heads only)*
½ *teaspoon freshly ground black pepper*
1 *tablespoon nori flakes for garnish*

In a large saucepan, sauté the leeks and scallions in the oils over medium-high heat for 5 minutes. Add the tamari, garlic, ginger, and tofu, and sauté another 3 minutes. Whisk in the miso paste and water. Add the remaining ingredients, except the nori flakes, reduce the heat to low, and let simmer for 50 minutes. Garnish with the nori flakes.

YIELD: 3 SERVINGS

Cream of Broccoli Soup

- 2 *cups soy milk*
- ¼ *cup cubed potatoes, steamed 15 minutes till tender*
- ½ *cup broccoli florets, steamed 4 minutes*
- ½ *vegetable bouillon cube (Morga)*
- 1 *cup water*
- ¼ *teaspoon freshly ground black pepper*
- 2 *tablespoons chopped fresh dill*
- 2 *tablespoons diced onions*
- 1 *teaspoon tamari*

Place all the ingredients in a blender and process until smooth. Pour into a medium-size saucepan and simmer over medium-low heat for 20 minutes.

YIELD: 2 SERVINGS

Cream of Broccoli Soup II

- 2 *tablespoons oil (sunflower, soy, or safflower)*
- 1 *cup chopped broccoli*
- 1 *vegetable bouillon cube dissolved in 1¼ cups water*
- 2 *cups soy milk*
- *Dash of ground nutmeg*
- ¼ *to ½ teaspoon salt*

Combine all the ingredients in a blender and process on high speed for 2 to 3 minutes until smooth. Pour the mixture into a medium-size saucepan, bring to a boil, then reduce the heat to medium and cover. Cook for 20 minutes, then serve hot.

YIELD: 2 SERVINGS

Lentil Pea Soup

- 1 *small yellow onion, chopped*
- 2 *cubed red or white potatoes*
- 1 *tablespoon extra virgin olive oil*
- 4 *cups water*
- 1/4 *cup dried yellow split peas, soaked in hot water and drained*
- 1/4 *cup dried red lentils, soaked in hot water till absorbed (about 30 minutes)*
- 1/2 *cup Brussels sprouts*
- 1/4 *cup chopped broccoli*
- 1/4 *cup sliced carrots*
- 1/4 *cup mixed frozen vegetables*
- 1 1/2 *teaspoons dulse*
- 1/8 *teaspoon salt*
- 1/8 *teaspoon freshly ground black pepper*
- 1/4 *teaspoon dried basil*
- 1/4 *teaspoon Herbimare*
- 1/4 *bay leaf*
- 1 1/2 *teaspoons curry powder*
- 1/4 *teaspoon dried rosemary*
- 1/4 *teaspoon dried thyme*
- 1/4 *teaspoon ground cumin*
- 1/4 *teaspoon minced green onions*

In a large saucepan, sauté the yellow onion and potatoes in the oil over medium-high heat for 5 to 7 minutes. Add the water, split peas, and lentils and cook over medium to low heat for 30 minutes. Add the remaining ingredients and cook another 20 minutes.

YIELD: 3 SERVINGS

Pea Soup

2 *cups frozen green peas*
½ *cup frozen corn*
1 *cup water*
½ *teaspoon freshly ground black pepper*
1 *vegetable bouillon cube (Morga)*
1 *teaspoon onion powder*
1 *teaspoon ground cumin*
Pinch of curry powder

Combine all the ingredients in a blender and process until smooth. Bring to a simmer over medium heat in a medium-size saucepan and serve hot or cold.

YIELD: 2 SERVINGS

Italian White Bean Soup

- ½ *cup chopped onions*
- 3 *cups chopped fresh tomatoes*
- ¼ *cup extra virgin olive oil*
- ½ *cup small bow-tie pasta*
- ¼ *cup chopped fresh parsley*
- 1 *cup canned white beans*
- 1¾ *teaspoons salt*
- ½ *teaspoon freshly ground black pepper*
- 2 *cups water*

In a medium-size saucepan, sauté the onions and tomatoes in the oil over medium-high heat for 5 to 7 minutes. Add the remaining ingredients, reduce the heat to medium-low, cover, and cook for an additional 20 to 40 minutes.

YIELD: 2 TO 3 SERVINGS

Creamy Potato Soup

½ *cup peeled, cubed potatoes*
¼ *cup sliced celery*
¼ *cup diced onions*
2 *tablespoons diced carrots*
1 *tablespoon safflower oil*
¼ *teaspoon salt*
Dash of freshly ground black pepper
1 *cup water*
1 *vegetable bouillon cube (Morga)*
1 *to 2 cups soy milk (depending on the consistency you like)*

In a large saucepan, sauté the potatoes, celery, onions, and carrots in the oil over medium-high heat for 7 to 8 minutes. Add the remaining ingredients and cook, covered, over medium to low heat for 25 to 30 minutes.

YIELD: 3 SERVINGS

Mock Chicken Tofu Soup

1	***vegetable bouillon cube (Morga)***
2¾	***cups water***
¼	***cup sliced scallions***
½	***cup sliced carrots***
1	***cup diced firm tofu***
¼	***teaspoon tamari***

In a medium-size saucepan, mix the vegetable bouillon with the water. Add the remaining ingredients and bring to a boil. Cover and cook over medium heat for 20 to 30 minutes.

YIELD: 2 TO 3 SERVINGS

Mock Chicken Gumbo

SOUP

- 4½ *teaspoons chopped fresh parsley*
- 4 *vegetable bouillon cubes (Morga) dissolved in ¼ cup hot water*
- ½ *cup sliced okra*
- 1½ *cups crushed tomatoes*
- 6 *cups water*
- 1 *teaspoon salt*
- ½ *teaspoon paprika*
- ½ *teaspoon freshly ground black pepper*
- 4½ *teaspoons extra virgin olive oil*
- ¼ *cup chopped onions*
- 1 *tablespoon hot sesame oil*

DUMPLINGS

- ¼ *teaspoon baking powder*
- 1¼ *cups flour (any type)*
- 1½ *teaspoons extra virgin olive oil*
- ½ *cup water*
- 4½ *teaspoons egg substitute or 1 medium egg*
- ½ *teaspoon salt*

In a large saucepan combine all the soup ingredients and cook over medium heat for one hour. In a medium-size mixing bowl, combine the baking powder and flour and mix well. Then add the remaining dumpling ingredients and combine thoroughly with a large spoon. Add teaspoonfuls of the dumpling mixture to the boiling soup, reduce heat to low, and cook an additional 10 minutes.

YIELD: 2 TO 3 SERVINGS

Chilled Cherry Soup

- ***1 cup apple juice***
- ***½ cup pitted, unsweetened cherries***
- ***1 cup unsweetened soy milk***
- ***1 cinnamon stick***

Combine all the ingredients except for the cinnamon stick in a blender and process on high speed until smooth. Pour the mixture into a medium-size saucepan, add the cinnamon stick, and bring to a simmer over medium to low heat. Cook an additional 2 to 3 minutes, until thick. Remove cinnamon stick. Chill 1 to 2 hours. Serve cold.

YIELD: 2 SERVINGS

[illegible]

Chilled Cherry Soup

[illegible]

[illegible]

CHAPTER 5

Salads

Romaine Sprout Salad

1 *cup sliced romaine lettuce*
½ *cup sliced radicchio*
1½ *cups sunflower sprouts*
2 *tablespoons sliced radishes*
½ *cup sliced cucumbers*
½ *cup sliced carrots*
½ *cup chopped fresh tomatoes*
2 *tablespoons chopped fresh dill*
2 *tablespoons chopped fresh basil*

Combine all the ingredients in a large salad bowl, toss with a vinaigrette dressing, and chill for one hour.

YIELD: 2 SERVINGS

Shelly's Caesar Salad

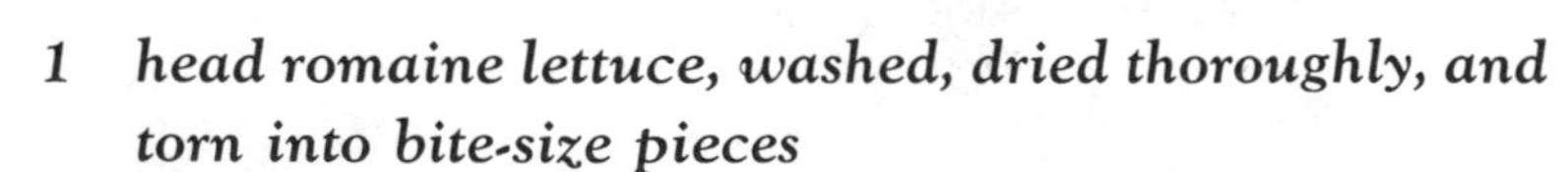

1 *head romaine lettuce, washed, dried thoroughly, and torn into bite-size pieces*
⅓ *cup extra virgin olive oil*
2 *cloves minced garlic*
1 *large egg, beaten*
¼ *cup grated Parmesan cheese*
½ *cup garlic croutons*
Dash of freshly ground black pepper

Place the lettuce in a medium-size bowl. Combine the oil and garlic in another bowl, then pour over the lettuce. Add the egg and mix a bit, then add the Parmesan and toss until thoroughly combined. Garnish with croutons and black pepper.

YIELD: 2 SERVINGS

Arugula–Red Pepper Salad

- 3/4 *cup sliced red bell peppers*
- 1 *cup sunflower sprouts*
- 1 *cup torn arugula*
- 3/4 *cup chopped fresh Italian parsley*
- 1 *cup shredded beets, steamed 15 minutes*
- 2/3 *cup shredded carrots*
- 1 *cup chopped fresh yellow tomatoes*

In a large salad bowl, combine all the ingredients, adding the tomatoes last as a garnish. Serve with a light lemon or vinaigrette dressing.

YIELD: 2 SERVINGS

Wilted Arugula with Oyster Mushrooms Parmesan

- 1/4 *cup extra virgin olive oil*
- 2 *cups stemmed oyster or shiitake mushrooms*
- 2 *to 3 1/4 tablespoons chopped fresh parsley*
- 1/8 *teaspoon salt*
- 5 *cups arugula*
- 1/4 *cup grated Parmesan cheese*
- 1/8 *teaspoon freshly ground black pepper*

In a large saucepan, saute the mushrooms, parsley, and salt in oil over medium heat, uncovered, for 3 to 4 minutes, being careful not to overcook. Turn off the heat and place the arugula leaves on top of the mushroom mixture and cover for 1 minute to wilt the leaves. Invert the pan onto a large plate and sprinkle on cheese and pepper and serve warm.

YIELD: 2 SERVINGS

Fresh Corn Salad

- 3 *cups corn kernels, steamed 10 minutes*
- 1 *cup chopped red bell pepper*
- 1 *cup chopped fennel, steamed 15 to 20 minutes*
- 1 *tablespoon finely chopped fresh coriander*
- 2 *tablespoons finely chopped fresh parsley*
- 2 *tablespoons extra virgin olive oil*
- 2 *tablespoons apple cider vinegar*
- ¼ *teaspoon salt*
- ⅛ *teaspoon freshly ground black pepper*

Combine all of the ingredients in a large bowl, toss, and serve cold or at room temperature.

YIELD: 2 SERVINGS

Curly Endive with Berries and Seeds

- 1 *cup torn curly or Belgian endive*
- ¼ *cup well-packed basil leaves*
- 1 *cup torn Bibb lettuce*
- ½ *cup sunflower sprouts*
- 1 *cup chopped fresh tomatoes or shredded carrots*
- 1 *cup blueberries*
- ½ *cup sunflower seeds*

Combine the endive, basil, lettuce, sprouts, and tomatoes in a large salad bowl. Garnish with the blueberries and seeds and serve with a favorite dressing like Orange Vinaigrette (see page 194).

YIELD: 2 SERVINGS

Broccoli Tortellini Salad

- 2 *cups uncooked tortellini*
- ½ *cup broccoli florets, steamed 3 to 4 minutes*
- ¼ *cup sliced black olives*
- ½ *cup sliced mushrooms*
- ½ *cup marinated artichoke hearts (jarred)*
- 3 *tablespoons apple cider vinegar*
- 1 *tablespoon tamari*

Place the tortellini in boiling water for 15 minutes, then drain and let cool for 10 minutes. Combine with the other ingredients in a medium-size bowl, then refrigerate for 2 hours before serving.

YIELD: 2 SERVINGS

Arame Cabbage Salad

- 3/4 *cup arame soaked in hot water, drained, and then measured*
- 1/2 *cup sliced purple cabbage*
- 1/2 *cup diced carrots*
- 1/4 *cup toasted sesame oil*
- 4 *to 6 tablespoons rice or apple cider vinegar*
- 1/4 *teaspoon salt*
- 1/4 *teaspoon freshly ground black pepper*
- 2 *tablespoons sesame seeds*

Combine all the ingredients in a large bowl. Mix well and chill for 1 hour before serving.

YIELD: 2 SERVINGS

Tangy Cucumber-Arame Salad

- 1 *cup sliced cucumbers*
- 1/2 *cup arame, soaked in hot water, drained, then measured*
- 1/2 *cup sliced red bell pepper*
- 1/4 *cup apple cider vinegar*
- 1/4 *cup sesame seeds*
- 3 *tablespoons oil (sunflower, soy, or safflower)*

Combine all the ingredients, toss, and serve.

YIELD: 2 SERVINGS

Tart Wakame-Cucumber Salad

- 1/3 *cup wakame, soaked, with tough stems removed*
- 1/4 *cup thinly sliced pickling cucumbers*
- 1/4 *cup thinly sliced lotus root*
- 1/2 *to 1 tablespoon balsamic vinegar*
- 2 *tablespoons black sesame seeds*

In a large salad bowl, combine the wakame, cucumbers, and lotus root. Toss in the vinegar, then sprinkle with the sesame seeds.

YIELD: 2 SERVINGS

French Mâche Salad

- 1 *cup mâche*
- 3 *spears asparagus, steamed and chilled*
- 1/4 *cup chopped fresh tomatoes*
- 1/4 *cup chopped carrots, steamed 5 to 10 minutes*
- 1/4 *cup Fresh Herb Vinaigrette (see page 194)*

Combine all of the ingredients, mix well, and chill.

YIELD: 1 SERVING

Artichoke-Chickpea Salad

- 1 *cup bulgur, soaked in hot water, then measured*
- ½ *cup marinated artichoke hearts (jarred)*
- ½ *cup dried chickpeas, soaked overnight in water and drained*
- ½ *cup chopped fresh parsley*
- ½ *cup chopped fresh dill*
- 2 *tablespoons chopped fresh mint*
- 1½ *teaspoons salt*
- ¼ *cup extra virgin olive oil*
- 1 *tablespoon fresh lemon juice*
- 1½ *teaspoons crushed garlic*
- 2 *tablespoons sliced scallions*
- ½ *cup chopped fresh tomatoes (optional)*

Combine all the ingredients in a large salad bowl. Mix well, chill, and serve.

YIELD: 2 SERVINGS

Beet and Bean Salad

- 1 *cup canned white navy beans*
- ½ *cup diced beets, steamed 15 minutes*
- ¾ *cup diced fennel*
- ⅓ *cup extra virgin olive oil*

2 *tablespoons chopped fresh basil*
1/8 *teaspoon dill seeds*
1 1/4 *teaspoons prepared mustard*
2 *to 3 tablespoons apple cider or balsamic vinegar*

Combine all the ingredients in a large salad bowl and toss. Chill for 1 to 2 hours, then serve.

YIELD: 2 SERVINGS

Mixed Beans Vinaigrette

1/2 *cup cooked lima beans*
1/2 *cup canned kidney beans, drained*
1/2 *cup green beans, steamed 15 minutes*
1/2 *cup chopped yellow bell pepper*
1/4 *cup chopped fresh parsley*
1 *to 2 tablespoons prepared mustard*
1 *to 2 tablespoons apple cider vinegar*
2 *tablespoons extra virgin olive oil*
1/4 *teaspoon freshly ground black pepper*
2 *tablespoons chopped red onions*

Combine all the ingredients in medium-size bowl, toss, and serve chilled.

YIELD: 2 SERVINGS

Four-Bean Salad

½ *cup green beans, steamed 15 minutes*
½ *cup fava beans, steamed 15 minutes*
½ *cup wax beans, steamed 10 minutes*
½ *cup Chinese long beans, steamed 10 minutes*
¼ *cup diced beets, steamed 15 minutes*
¼ *cup diced carrots*
1 *cup currants*
¼ *cup extra virgin olive oil*
2½ *tablespoons fresh lemon juice*
1 *tablespoon chopped fresh basil*
1 *tablespoon chopped fresh mint*
½ *teaspoon salt*
½ *teaspoon freshly ground black pepper*

In a large salad bowl, combine all the ingredients, toss well, and chill one hour before serving.

YIELD: 2 SERVINGS

Sesame Bean Salad

½ *cup canned chickpeas*
½ *cup canned black beans*
½ *cup canned kidney beans*
¼ *cup sliced scallions*

1 cup seeded orange segments
3 tablespoons orange juice
4½ teaspoons fresh lemon juice
¼ cup toasted sesame oil
½ cup sesame seeds
1 teaspoon salt
½ teaspoon freshly ground black pepper

Combine all the ingredients in a large salad bowl. Mix well and chill for one hour before serving.

YIELD: 2 SERVINGS

Cold German Leek Salad

½ cup sliced beets, steamed 15 minutes
1 cup sliced carrots, steamed 15 minutes
2 cups sliced leeks, steamed 10 minutes
2 tablespoons prepared mustard
½ cup extra virgin olive oil
1 tablespoon fresh lemon juice
2 tablespoons chopped fresh parsley
2 tablespoons chopped fresh dill

In a large salad bowl, combine all the ingredients, tossing well. Chill for one hour before serving.

YIELD: 2 SERVINGS

Shelly's Potato Salad

- 4 *(2 cups) red potatoes, steamed 15 to 20 minutes and sliced*
- 1 *cup sliced hard-boiled eggs*
- ¼ *cup chopped fresh parsley*
- 2 *tablespoons chopped fresh basil*
- ½ *cup diced onions*
- 2 *tablespoons prepared mustard*
- ½ *cup apple cider vinegar*
- ¼ *cup extra virgin olive oil*
- 1 *tablespoon chopped fresh dill*
- ½ *teaspoon salt*
- ¼ *teaspoon freshly ground black pepper*

Combine all the ingredients in a medium-size bowl. Toss and serve at room temperature or chilled.

YIELD: 2 SERVINGS

Fresh Tuna Salad

- 1 *cup broiled fresh tuna cubes*
- ¼ *cup toasted sesame oil*
- ¼ *cup sliced scallions*
- 1 *tablespoon fresh lemon juice*
- 1 *orange, seeded and in segments*

- ¼ cup chopped fresh parsley
- ½ to 1 teaspoon salt
- 1 teaspoon freshly ground black pepper

Combine all the ingredients in a large bowl. Mix well and chill for one hour before serving.

YIELD: 2 SERVINGS

Vegetable Tofu Salad

- 1 package silken tofu, diced
- ½ cup diced carrots, steamed 15 minutes
- ½ cup chopped snow peas
- 6 tablespoons chopped fresh parsley
- 6 to 8 tablespoons sesame oil
- 1 tablespoon curry powder
- ½ to 1 tablespoon salt
- 1½ teaspoons freshly ground black pepper
- 2 tablespoons sliced scallions
- ½ cup raisins

In a large salad bowl, combine the tofu, carrots, snow peas, and parsley. Add the sesame oil, mix well, then stir in the curry powder, salt, and pepper. Make sure salad is mixed well before tossing in the scallions and raisins. Serve chilled and with bread or crackers.

YIELD: 2 SERVINGS

Couscous Sprout Salad

2 *cups cooked couscous*
½ *cup diced carrots*
¼ *cup chopped fresh parsley*
½ *cup cooked fava or lima beans*
3 *tablespoons tamari*
2 *tablespoons raisins*
½ *cup alfalfa or radish sprouts*
3 *tablespoons extra virgin olive oil*
¼ *teaspoon freshly ground black pepper*
2 *tablespoons sliced scallions*

Combine all the ingredients in a medium-size bowl, toss, and serve at room temperature.

YIELD: 2 SERVINGS

Japanese Buckwheat Salad

3 *cups cooked buckwheat noodles*
¼ *cup toasted sesame oil*
2 *tablespoons sliced scallions*
2 *tablespoons raisins*
2 *tablespoons sunflower seeds*
1 *cup broccoli florets, steamed 5 to 6 minutes*

1 *cup sliced carrots*
3 *to 4 tablespoons tamari*
¼ *cup gomasio*

Combine all the ingredients in a medium-size bowl and mix well. Serve chilled.

YIELD: 2 SERVINGS

Amaranth Salad

3 *cups cooked amaranth*
2 *tablespoons sunflower, soy, or safflower oil*
2 *tablespoons chopped fresh parsley*
4 *to 6 tablespoons tamari*
2 *tablespoons currants*
3 *tablespoons chopped fresh mint*
2 *tablespoons sliced scallions*
2 *tablespoons fresh lemon juice*
2 *tablespoons chopped garlic*

Combine all the ingredients in a medium-size bowl, mix well, chill, and serve.

YIELD: 2 SERVINGS

Crunchy Apple Rice Salad

1 *cup uncooked long-grain brown rice*
½ *cup uncooked wild rice*
3 *cups water*
1 *tablespoon sunflower or safflower oil*
2 *tablespoons ground cinnamon*
½ *cup chopped apples*
¼ *cup chopped fresh parsley*
¾ *cup currants or raisins*

Combine the rices, water, oil, and cinnamon in a medium-size saucepan over medium heat. Cook until the water is absorbed, about 15 to 20 minutes. Turn off the heat and cover for five minutes. Put the rice mixture in a large salad bowl and toss in the apples, parsley, and currants. Serve hot or cold.

YIELD: 2 SERVINGS

Fabulous Wild Rice Salad

3 *cups cooked wild rice*
½ *cup sliced carrots*
½ *cup broccoli florets, steamed 5 to 6 minutes*
½ *cup chopped fresh parsley*
½ *cup diced zucchini*
3 *tablespoons safflower oil*

1 *teaspoon chopped fresh dill*
2 *tablespoons fresh lemon juice*
¼ *teaspoon freshly ground black pepper*
½ *teaspoon salt*

Combine all the ingredients in a medium-size bowl, mix well, toss, and serve at room temperature.

YIELD: 2 SERVINGS

Fennel and Pecan Salad

1 *cup sliced fennel root*
1½ *cups well-packed dandelion greens*
½ *cup well-packed Italian parsley leaves*
½ *cup diced fresh peaches*
¼ *cup chopped pecans*
½ *cup pomegranate seeds (optional)*

Combine the fennel, dandelion greens, parsley, and peaches in a large salad bowl. Toss with a light, sweet salad dressing, like Orange Vinaigrette (see page 194), and top with the pecans and pomegranate seeds. Serve chilled.

YIELD: 2 SERVINGS

Mixed Sprout, Bean, and Nut Salad

- 2 *cups sunflower sprouts*
- 2 *cups alfalfa sprouts*
- ½ *cup radish sprouts*
- ¼ *cup canned garbanzo beans*
- ½ *cup asparagus tips, steamed 8 to 10 minutes*
- ½ *cup avocado cubes*
- ¼ *cup halved seedless grapes*
- ¼ *cup chopped Brazil nuts*

Combine all the ingredients in a large salad bowl and chill for 1 hour. Serve with Lime Vinaigrette (see page 193) or the dressing of your choice.

YIELD: 2 SERVINGS

Chinese Sprout Salad

- 1½ *cups whole walnuts*
- ½ *cup honey*
- 3 *cups sliced green cabbage*
- 1 *cup sliced nori*
- 2 *cups bean sprouts*

1	*cup diced raw carrots*
½	*cup sesame seeds*
	Sweet and Sour Salad Dressing (see page 199)

Coat the walnuts with the honey and bake in a preheated 375°F oven for 20 minutes on a lightly greased cookie sheet. Toss the cabbage, nori, bean sprouts, carrots, and sesame seeds in a large bowl, then toss with the dressing, top with the walnuts, and serve.

YIELD: 2 SERVINGS

The Very Best Fruit Salad

½	*cup peeled, sliced fresh peaches*
½	*cup fresh raspberries*
¼	*cup sliced fresh figs (optional)*
½	*cup sliced kiwi fruit*
½	*cup chopped mango*
½	*cup fresh blackberries*
¼	*cup fresh lime juice*
½	*cup white grape juice*
	Fresh mint leaves for garnish

Combine all the ingredients in a large serving bowl, tossing well, and garnish with the mint.

YIELD: 2 TO 3 SERVINGS

Herb Croutons

- 1½ *cups toasted or day-old bread cubes (any type)*
- ¼ *cup extra virgin olive oil*
- 1 *tablespoon dried basil*
- 1½ *teaspoons dried thyme*
- 1½ *teaspoons dried sage*

In a medium-size bowl, toss the bread cubes with the oil and herbs. Bake on a cookie sheet in a preheated 375°F oven for 15 to 20 minutes or until brown. Serve directly in salads or place in a plastic bag in the refrigerator for storage up to one week.

YIELD: ABOUT 1½ CUPS CROUTONS

SPICY SESAME CROUTONS: Use ½ teaspoon hot sesame oil, ¼ cup sesame seeds, and 2 tablespoons nori or kelp flakes instead of the olive oil and herbs.

CHAPTER 6

Rice and Grains

Mrs. Kartalyan's Rice Pilaf

2 *cups water*
1/4 *to 3/4 teaspoon saffron threads*
1 *cup uncooked brown rice*
1/2 *cup tiny uncooked pasta, in the shape of your choice*
1/2 *cup sliced almonds*
6 *tablespoons margarine or oil*
1 *bay leaf*

Bring 1/2 cup of the water to a boil. Add the saffron and let sit for 15 minutes. Meanwhile, in a large saucepan, sauté the rice, pasta, and almonds in the margarine over medium heat until the mixture turns light brown. Then add the saffron water, the remaining water, and the bay leaf. Bring to a boil, then reduce the heat to low and let cook, covered, until the water is almost absorbed, about 15 to 20 minutes. Turn off the heat and let sit for 5 minutes.

YIELD: 2 SERVINGS

Risotto with Shiitake Mushrooms Parmesan

- 3 ½ *cups soy or regular milk*
- ½ *cup stemmed and sliced shiitake mushrooms*
- ½ *cup arborio rice*
- 1 *tablespoon finely chopped fresh Italian parsley*
- ¼ *cup grated Parmesan cheese*
- ⅛ *teaspoon freshly ground black pepper*

In a saucepan, bring the milk to a simmer over low heat, being careful not to boil. Stir in the mushrooms and rice and cook for 20 to 25 minutes or till creamy. Add the remaining ingredients and cook an additional 1 to 2 minutes over a low flame. Serve hot.

YIELD: 2 SERVINGS

Risotto with Tomatoes and Peas

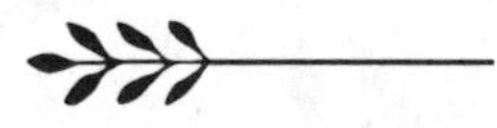

- 3 ½ *cups milk*
- ½ *cup arborio rice*
- ¼ *cup chopped fresh tomatoes*
- ¼ *cup frozen or canned peas*
- 1 *tablespoon finely chopped fresh Italian parsley*

¼ *teaspoon salt*
⅛ *teaspoon freshly ground black pepper*
⅛ *teaspoon grated Parmesan cheese*

In a saucepan, bring the milk to a simmer over low heat, being careful not to boil. Add the rice and tomatoes and cook uncovered for 10 minutes. Add the remaining ingredients and cook an additional 10 to 15 minutes till creamy. Serve hot with the Parmesan cheese on top and a salad on the side.

YIELD: 2 SERVINGS

Mushroom and Pea Biryani

½ *cup fresh or frozen peas*
1 *large yellow onion, chopped*
½ *cup sliced mushrooms (shiitake, if possible)*
1 *bay leaf*
1½ *teaspoons salt*
¼ *teaspoon freshly ground black pepper*
3 *tablespoons vegetable oil*
3 *cups cooked brown basmati rice*
¼ *teaspoon ground cardamom*
2 *teaspoons ground coriander*
⅛ *teaspoon ground ginger*
½ *teaspoon ground nutmeg*
1 *cinnamon stick*

In a large saucepan, sauté the peas, onions, and mushrooms with the bay leaf, salt, and pepper in the oil over medium-high heat until the onions are clear. Drain any excess water the mushrooms may have thrown off. Stir in the rice and spices and cook until hot over medium heat. Remove cinnamon stick before serving.

YIELD: 2 SERVINGS

Vegetable Biryani

- ¾ *teaspoon saffron threads*
- 2 *tablespoons water*
- 3 *cups cooked brown basmati rice*
- ½ *cup cauliflower florets, steamed 10 minutes*
- 2 *tablespoons diced carrots, steamed 10 to 15 minutes*
- ¼ *cup fresh or frozen green beans*
- ¼ *cup whole cashews*
- ¼ *cup sliced almonds*
- 2 *tablespoons raisins*
- 2 *whole nutmegs*
- 1 *cinnamon stick*
- ¼ *teaspoon freshly ground black pepper*
- 1½ *teaspoons salt*
- 4½ *teaspoons vegetable oil*

Soak the saffron in the water for 10 to 15 minutes, then stir into the rice. In a large saucepan, sauté the rice and remaining ingredients over medium heat until hot. Remove the whole spices before serving.

YIELD: 2 SERVINGS

Lentils and Rice with Thyme

½ *cup sliced cooked carrots*
¾ *cup chopped onions*
¼ *cup sliced celery*
1 *teaspoon dried sage*
1 *teaspoon dried thyme*
1 *teaspoon chopped garlic*
2 *teaspoons oil (sunflower, soy, or safflower)*
1 *cup cooked lentils*
1 *cup cooked long-grain brown rice*

In a large saucepan, sauté the carrots, onions, and celery with the herbs and garlic in the oil over medium heat until the onions are clear. Add the lentils and rice and warm through.

YIELD: 2 TO 3 SERVINGS

Red Brazilian Rice

- 1/4 *cup chopped red onions*
- 1 *fresh tomato, chopped or 1/2 cup prepared tomato sauce*
- 1 1/2 *teaspoons drained, crushed capers*
- 2 *tablespoons sliced large green olives*
- 1 *bay leaf*
- 2 *tablespoons extra virgin olive oil*
- 3 *cups cooked white basmati rice*
- 2 *tablespoons pumpkin seeds*
- 1/4 *teaspoon dried thyme*
- 1/2 *teaspoon freshly ground black pepper*
- 1 *teaspoon salt*

In a large saucepan, sauté the onions, tomatoes, capers, olives, and bay leaf in oil over medium heat until the onions are clear. Add the remaining ingredients and sauté another 3 to 4 minutes, until hot. Serve with black beans.

YIELD: 2 SERVINGS

Cold Armenian Rice with Leeks

- 1 *white or yellow onion, chopped*
- 2 *large carrots, sliced*

- ⅓ *cup extra virgin olive oil*
- 8 *leeks, sliced*
- 1¾ *cups uncooked short-grain brown rice*
- ⅓ *cup chopped fresh parsley*
- 1 *tablespoon salt*
- 2 *teaspoons freshly ground black pepper*
- 4 *cups water*
- 1 *lemon, cut into wedges for garnish*

In a large saucepan, sauté the onions and carrots in the oil over medium heat until the onions are clear. Stir in the leeks, then add the remaining ingredients, except the lemon, cover, and cook over low heat until almost all the water is absorbed, about 15 to 20 minutes. Turn off the heat and let stand 5 minutes. Serve cold with lemon wedges.

YIELD: 2 SERVINGS

Basmati Rice with Peppers and Fresh Herbs

- 1½ *cups cooked brown basmati rice*
- ¾ *tablespoon chopped fresh marjoram*
- ½ *teaspoon chopped fresh tarragon*
- 1 *to 2 tablespoons diced red bell pepper*
- 1 *to 2 tablespoons diced yellow bell pepper*
- 1 *to 2 tablespoons diced green bell pepper*
- ¼ *teaspoon salt*
- ¼ *teaspoon freshly ground black pepper*
- 1½ *tablespoons butter*

In a large saucepan, combine all the ingredients and sauté in the butter for 10 to 15 minutes on medium heat.

YIELD: 2 SERVINGS

Peanut Thai Rice Sauté

- 4½ *teaspoons peanut oil*
- ¼ *cup chopped zucchini*
- ¼ *cup chopped green onions*
- ½ *teaspoon chopped shallots*
- ¼ *cup chopped unsalted roasted peanuts*
- 3 *cups cooked long-grain brown rice*
- 1 *tablespoon chopped fresh cilantro*
- 1½ *teaspoons chopped garlic*
- 4½ *teaspoons chopped fresh mint for garnish*

Heat the peanut oil in a skillet or wok until hot, but not smoking, over high heat. Add the zucchini, onions, and shallots, and sauté over medium-high heat for 3 to 5 minutes. Add the remaining ingredients one at a time, stirring after each addition, and cook until hot. Garnish with chopped mint.

YIELD: 2 SERVINGS

Millet-Coriander Stir-fry

½ *cup sliced daikon*
½ *cup sliced carrots*
½ *cup sliced zucchini*
3 *tablespoons sesame oil*
3 *cups cooked millet*
3 *tablespoons tamari*
½ *teaspoon grated fresh ginger*
1 *teaspoon chopped garlic*
2 *tablespoons sesame seeds*
2 *tablespoons chopped fresh parsley*
1 *tablespoon chopped fresh coriander*

Sauté the daikon, carrots, and zucchini in the oil in a large saucepan over medium heat for 5 to 8 minutes. Add the remaining ingredients, mix well, and sauté an additional 3 to 6 minutes. Serve hot.

YIELD: 2 SERVINGS

Sesame Amaranth with Broccoli

½ *cup broccoli florets*
½ *cup sliced mushrooms (shiitake or enoki)*
½ *cup sliced carrots or butternut squash, steamed 15 minutes*
½ *cup cauliflower florets, steamed 10 minutes*
3 *tablespoons sesame oil*
3 *cups cooked amaranth*
2 *tablespoons sliced scallions*
1 *tablespoon chopped garlic*
2 *tablespoons tamari*
¼ *cup sesame seeds*

Sauté the broccoli, mushrooms, carrots, and cauliflower in the oil in a large saucepan over medium heat for 3 to 5 minutes. Add the remaining ingredients, mix well, and cook an additional 2 to 3 minutes.

YIELD: 2 SERVINGS

Oriental Amaranth with Purple Cabbage

½ *cup sliced red bell peppers*
½ *cup sliced purple cabbage*

- ½ *cup Brussels sprouts*
- 3 *tablespoons toasted sesame oil*
- 3 *tablespoons tamari*
- 2 *tablespoons gomasio*
- 1 *cup cooked amaranth*
- 2 *tablespoons chopped fresh parsley*

In a medium-size saucepan, sauté the peppers, cabbage, and sprouts in the oil over medium heat for 3 to 5 minutes. Add the remaining ingredients, mix well, and cook an additional 3 to 6 minutes.

YIELD: 2 SERVINGS

Apple Walnut Millet

- 1½ *cups uncooked millet*
- 1½ *cups water*
- ½ *cup chopped walnuts, blanched (see note below)*
- ¼ *cup chopped dried apple*

Bring the millet and water to a boil in small saucepan, then reduce the heat to low. Stirring occasionally, cook for 30 minutes, then add the remaining ingredients, mix well, and warm through.

YIELD: 2 SERVINGS

Note: To blanch nuts, bring to a boil with enough water to cover, then drain immediately.

Barley with Collard Greens and Leeks

½ *cup sliced leeks*
½ *cup sliced mushrooms*
1 *cup sliced collard greens*
1 *cup chopped fresh tomatoes*
2 *tablespoons extra virgin olive oil*
3 *cups cooked barley*
½ *cup sliced red bell peppers*
¼ *cup chopped fresh parsley*
1 *teaspoon celery salt*
½ *teaspoon freshly ground black pepper*
½ *teaspoon dried oregano*

In a large saucepan, sauté the leeks, mushrooms, collard greens, and tomatoes in the oil over medium heat for 5 minutes. Add the remaining ingredients, mix well, and sauté an additional 3 to 5 minutes.

YIELD: 2 SERVINGS

Singapore Brown Rice

½ *cup diced firm tofu*
¼ *cup sliced scallions*

2 *tablespoons diced carrots*
¼ *cup frozen peas*
2 *tablespoons canned bamboo shoots*
2 *tablespoons canned sliced water chestnuts*
6 *cups cooked long-grain brown rice*
2 *tablespoons soy sauce or tamari*
1 *teaspoon finely chopped fresh coriander*
2 *tablespoons sesame oil*

In a large saucepan, sauté all the ingredients over medium heat, adding them in the order in which they are listed, until hot.

YIELD: 2 SERVINGS

Wild Rice with Spinach and Cream

1 *cup uncooked long-grain rice*
2 *cups water*
1 *vegetable bouillon cube (Morga)*
½ *cup cooked wild rice*
½ *cup chopped onions*
1 *cup sliced celery*
1 *cup sliced mushrooms*
2 *tablespoons chopped fresh thyme*
3 *tablespoons extra virgin olive oil*
1 *cup torn spinach*
½ *cup soy milk*
½ *teaspoon salt*

Cook the long-grain rice in the water, first dissolving the bouillon cube in it. Then sauté both the rices with the onions, celery, mushrooms, and thyme in the oil over medium heat till the onions are clear. Combine the spinach, milk, and salt in a blender and puree. Pour this over the rice mixture, mix well, and serve.

YIELD: 2 TO 3 SERVINGS

Tomato Rice with Black Beans

- ¾ *cup chopped onions*
- 3 *cups chopped fresh tomatoes*
- 1½ *cups frozen peas*
- 6 *tablespoons extra virgin olive oil*
- ½ *teaspoon salt*
- ¼ *teaspoon freshly ground black pepper*
- 1½ *tablespoons turmeric*
- 1½ *to 2 cups canned black beans*
- 5½ *cups cooked short-grain brown rice or wild rice blend*

In a large saucepan, combine the onions, tomatoes, peas, oil, salt, and pepper and cook over medium-high heat, covered, for 5 to 7 minutes until it thickens. Stir in the turmeric, beans, and rice and heat through.

YIELD: 3 SERVINGS

CHAPTER 7

Side Dishes

Stewed Green Cabbage with Corn and Peas

- 5 *cups chopped green cabbage*
- 2 *cups water*
- 1/4 *cup sliced onions*
- 2 *tablespoons caraway seeds*
- 3/4 *to 1 1/2 teaspoons salt*
- 1/4 *teaspoon freshly ground black pepper*
- 1/4 *cup frozen peas*
- 1/4 *cup frozen corn*
- 1 *tablespoon curry powder*

In a large saucepan, combine all the ingredients and bring to a boil. Reduce heat to medium-low and cook for an additional 25 to 30 minutes. Serve hot or cold.

YIELD: 2 TO 4 SERVINGS

Vegetable-stuffed Artichokes

- 2 *artichokes*
- 2 *cups water*
- 2 *tablespoons plus 1 teaspoon fresh lemon juice*
- 2 *artichoke hearts, chopped*
- 1/4 *cup chopped avocado*
- 1/4 *cup chopped fresh tomatoes*
- 3 *tablespoons chopped black olives*
- 1 *tablespoon chopped onions*
- 2 *tablespoons extra virgin olive oil*
- 2 *tablespoons chopped fresh basil*
- 1/2 *teaspoon salt*
- 1 *lemon, sliced, for garnish*

Trim the thorns from the artichoke leaves with a pair of scissors and trim the bottoms so they will stand upright. In a medium-size saucepan, simmer the artichokes in the water and 4 teaspoons of the lemon juice over medium heat. The artichokes are done when the leaves pull out easily, about 50 to 60 minutes. Remove from the water and let cool. Gently pull out the center leaves and scoop out the fuzzy choke with a spoon. Combine the remaining ingredients in a small mixing bowl and stir well. Spoon the stuffing mixture into the centers of the artichokes and garnish with lemon slices.

YIELD: 2 SERVINGS

Japanese Hijiki

1 *cup hijiki, soaked in water and drained*
2 *tablespoons toasted sesame oil*
2 *tablespoons finely chopped scallions*
2 *tablespoons diced red bell pepper*
1 *tablespoon tamari*

Sauté the above ingredients in a skillet over medium heat for 5 minutes and serve at room temperature. This can be stored for up to two days in the refrigerator and served cold.

YIELD: 2 SERVINGS (1¼ CUPS)

Mr. Kartalyan's Chilled Cucumbers with Dill

1 *cup peeled, seeded, and sliced cucumbers*
2 *cups plain yogurt*
2 *tablespoons chopped fresh dill*
2 *tablespoons extra virgin olive oil*
½ *teaspoon crushed garlic*

Combine all the ingredients in a medium-size bowl and mix well. Chill for 1 to 2 hours before serving.

YIELD: 2 SERVINGS

Sautéed Kale with Black-eyed Peas

- 1 *cup finely chopped kale, steamed 5 minutes*
- ½ *cup diced apples*
- 1 *cup sliced mushrooms*
- ½ *cup sliced fennel root*
- ¾ *teaspoon salt*
- ¼ *teaspoon freshly ground black pepper*
- 2 *tablespoons extra virgin olive oil*
- ½ *cup black-eyed peas, steamed 15 minutes*
- 4½ *teaspoons apple juice*
- 2¼ *teaspoons ground cinnamon*
- 2 *tablespoons chopped fresh cilantro*
- 2 *tablespoons chopped fresh parsley*
- ¾ *to 1 teaspoon ground nutmeg*

In a large saucepan, sauté the kale, apples, mushrooms, fennel, salt, and pepper in the oil over medium-high heat for 5 to 8 minutes. Add the remaining ingredients and cook an additional 5 to 8 minutes. Serve hot.

YIELD: 2 SERVINGS

Old-fashioned Baked Beans

- 3 *cups cooked Great Northern beans*
- 6 *cups water*

3½ *tablespoons ketchup*
¼ *teaspoon dry mustard*
4½ *teaspoons unsulfured molasses*
1½ *teaspoons date sugar*

Combine all the ingredients in a medium-size baking dish and bake, uncovered, in a preheated 425°F oven for 1 to 1½ hours.

YIELD: 2 SERVINGS

Okra Cornmeal Fritters

½ *cup cornmeal*
½ *teaspoon salt*
½ *teaspoon freshly ground black pepper*
1 *cup small whole okra*
1 *large egg, beaten*
½ *cup whole wheat flour*
¼ *cup safflower oil*

Combine the cornmeal, salt, and pepper in a small bowl and mix well. Dip the okra into the egg, then the cornmeal mixture, then into the wheat flour. The coating should be light. Fry in the oil over medium-high heat until crispy, 5 to 6 minutes. Drain the fried okra on paper towels.

YIELD: 2 SERVINGS

Cranberry-Stuffed Pumpkins

1½ cups stemmed and sliced brown crimini or shiitake mushrooms
1 cup Holiday Cranberry Sauce (see page 108)
2 tablespoons chopped fresh parsley
3 tablespoons fresh lemon juice
1 cup apple juice
1 small pumpkin, halved and cleaned
½ cup maple or date sugar
1 teaspoon grated lemon rind

In a medium-size bowl, combine the mushrooms, cranberry sauce, parsley, lemon juice, and apple juice and mix well. Stuff into the pumpkin halves, then place in a baking dish. Bake, covered, in a preheated 425°F oven for one hour. Mix together the maple sugar and lemon rind and sprinkle over the pumpkin halves. Bake, uncovered, an additional 15 minutes.

YIELD: 2 SERVINGS

Sweet Cabbage and Apple Casserole

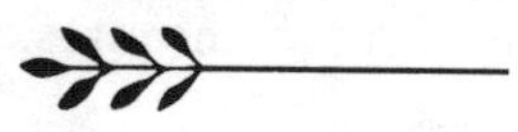

1 cup sliced celery
1 cup sliced green cabbage
2 cups chopped apples

- ½ *cup chopped onions*
- 1 *tablespoon apple cider vinegar*
- 2 *tablespoons ground allspice*
- ½ *cup apple juice*
- ½ *cup chopped prunes*
- 1½ *teaspoons caraway seeds*

In a large saucepan, sauté the celery, cabbage, apples, and onions in the vinegar over medium-high heat for 5 minutes. Stir in the allspice, juice, prunes, and caraway seeds. Place in a baking dish and bake in a preheated 375°F oven for 30 minutes.

YIELD: 2 TO 4 SERVINGS

Grandma's Green Beans

- ½ *cup diced yellow onions*
- ¼ *cup extra virgin olive oil*
- 1 *cup chopped fresh tomatoes*
- 4 *cups fresh green beans, strings removed*
- ½ *teaspoon salt*
- ¼ *teaspoon freshly ground black pepper*
- 2 *tablespoons chopped fresh parsley*
- 1 *cup water*

In a large saucepan, sauté the onions in the oil for 5 minutes. Add the remaining ingredients and cook, covered, for 1 hour over medium-low heat.

YIELD: 2 SERVINGS

Fresh Green Beans with Onions and Herbs

- 1/4 *cup extra virgin olive oil*
- 3 *cups fresh green beans, steamed 5 minutes*
- 1/4 *cup chopped fresh parsley*
- 2 *to 4 tablespoons chopped onions*
- 1/4 *cup chopped almonds*
- 1/4 *cup chopped hazelnuts*
- 1/4 *cup sunflower seeds*
- 1/4 *cup chopped walnuts*
- 2 *tablespoons chopped fresh chervil*
- 2 *to 4 tablespoons dill seed*
- 2 *to 4 tablespoons chopped fresh dill*
- 2 *tablespoons chopped shallots*
- *Herb Croutons (see page 78) for garnish*

In a large bowl, combine all the ingredients, garnishing with the Herb Croutons.

YIELD: 2 SERVINGS

Butternut Squash with Toasted Sesame Sauce

1 *butternut squash, cut into ½-inch pieces*
2 *tablespoons toasted sesame oil*
6 *to 8 tablespoons tahini*
3 *to 4 tablespoons gomasio*

Steam the squash for 15 to 20 minutes. Remove from the heat and divide into two or three portions. Combine the oil and tahini in a small bowl and mix well. Pour the tahini mixture over the squash. Sprinkle with gomasio.

YIELD: 2 TO 3 SERVINGS

Yellow Squash with Creamy Dill Sauce

2 *cups sliced yellow squash*
2 *tablespoons butter or oil (sunflower, soy, or safflower)*
3½ *tablespoons soy milk*
2 *tablespoons chopped fresh dill*
½ *teaspoon salt*
Dash of apple cider vinegar
1 *cup plain yogurt*

In a large saucepan, sauté the squash in the butter over medium heat for 5 minutes. Remove to a baking dish. Combine the remaining ingredients and pour over the squash. Bake in a preheated 375°F oven for 20 to 25 minutes.

YIELD: 2 SERVINGS

Cinnamon Apples with Spaghetti Squash

- 2 *medium-size spaghetti squash, halved*
- 1 *cup chopped apples*
- ½ *cup raisins*
- 2 *teaspoons ground cinnamon*
- ½ *cup pure maple syrup*
- ½ *cup chopped almonds*

Steam the halved squash until done, about 15 minutes. It is done when a strand of spaghetti can be removed easily by scraping the squash with a spoon. Dice the squash, then toss in the remaining ingredients and serve hot.

YIELD: 2 SERVINGS

Oshitoshi

- 1 *bunch (40 stalks) watercress*
- 1 *tablespoon tamari*
- 3 *tablespoons water*
- 2 *tablespoons mirin (optional)*
- 2 *teaspoons sesame seeds*

Steam the watercress stalks for 1 to 2 minutes. Combine the tamari, water, and mirin in a small bowl, then pour over the watercress and garnish with the sesame seeds.

YIELD: 2 SERVINGS

Sautéed Dandelion Greens with Corn and Red Peppers

- 4 *cups dandelion greens*
- ¼ *cup extra virgin olive oil*
- ½ *cup cooked fresh corn off the cob*
- ¾ *cup sliced red bell peppers*
- ½ *teaspoon salt*
- ¼ *teaspoon freshly ground black pepper*
- 1 *tablespoon chopped fresh basil*

Combine all the ingredients in a large saucepan over medium heat and cook for 10 to 15 minutes until the dandelion greens wilt.

YIELD: 2 TO 4 SERVINGS

Holiday Cranberry Sauce

- 1/3 *cup kudzu pieces*
- 6 *cups water*
- 1 *12-ounce package fresh cranberries, washed*
- 2 *cups maple sugar*
- 1 *tablespoon grated orange rind*

Dissolve the kudzu in 1 cup of the water in a large saucepan. Add the cranberries to the kudzu mixture, then the remaining ingredients. Cook for 30 minutes over high heat or until the cranberries crack open and the mixture is uniform. Strain the mixture through a sieve and chill 2 to 3 hours.

YIELD: 3 CUPS

Sweet Cranberry Ginger Toss

- 1 *cup fresh cranberries, steamed 20 minutes or till they crack open*
- 1 *tablespoon sesame oil*

¼ *cup fresh lemon juice*
2 *tablespoons pure maple syrup*
1 *teaspoon grated fresh ginger*
1 *tablespoon grated orange rind*

Combine all the ingredients in a bowl and mix well. Serve with Sweet Autumn Casserole (see page 134) or yams.

YIELD: 2 SERVINGS

Christmas Sauté

4 *cups sliced celery*
1 *cup whole almonds, blanched*
2 *tablespoons sesame oil*
¾ *cup fresh cranberries*
2 *tablespoons grated fresh ginger*
½ *cup date sugar*
2 *tablespoons sesame seeds*

In a large saucepan, sauté the celery and almonds in the oil for 3 to 5 minutes over medium heat. Add the cranberries and ginger, and sauté another 3 to 5 minutes. Stir in the sugar and garnish with the sesame seeds.

YIELD: 2 TO 3 SERVINGS

Apple-Parsley Stuffing

2 *cups sliced apples, steamed 10 minutes*
¼ *cup raisins*
4 *cups packaged bread cubes for stuffing, soaked in water according to package instructions*
½ *cup chopped pecans or chestnuts*
¼ *cup fresh cranberries, steamed 15 minutes*
¼ *cup chopped fresh parsley*
2 *to 4 tablespoons pure maple syrup*
½ *teaspoon ground allspice*
1 *large egg (only add if making a loaf)*

Combine all the ingredients in a medium-size bowl and mix well. Place inside the bird and bake, or add the egg and pour into a greased loaf pan and bake in a preheated 375°F oven for 25 to 30 minutes, covered.

YIELD: 6 CUPS

Chestnut-Mushroom Stuffing

½ *cup diced mushrooms*
2 *tablespoons chopped fresh parsley*
2 *tablespoons chopped onions*
1 *bay leaf*
¼ *cup extra virgin olive oil*
½ *cup cubed chestnuts*

1 *cup packaged bread cubes for stuffing, soaked in water according to package instructions*
1 *tablespoon dried sage*
1 *tablespoon dried rosemary*
1 *tablespoon dried thyme*

Sauté the mushrooms, parsley, onions, and bay leaf in the oil in a large saucepan over medium-high heat for 5 minutes. Combine the remaining ingredients in a medium-size bowl, then toss in the sautéed mixture. Place in a greased baking dish and bake in a preheated 425°F oven for 30 minutes.

YIELD: 3 SERVINGS

Squash Stuffing

1 *cup chopped butternut squash*
½ *cup chopped apples*
½ *cup chopped pears*
¼ *cup chopped walnuts*
¼ *cup golden raisins*
1 *tablespoon ground allspice*
1 *teaspoon ground cinnamon*

Steam the butternut squash for 15 to 20 minutes. Then combine with the remaining ingredients. Toss well and serve at room temperature as a side dish to a holiday dinner, or use as a stuffing for a small turkey.

YIELD: 2 SERVINGS

Caraway Apples

½ *to ¾ cup water*
1 *cup sliced McIntosh apples*
1 *cup sliced carrots*
2 *tablespoons caraway seeds*
3 *tablespoons butter*
4½ *teaspoons pure maple syrup*
⅛ *to ¼ teaspoon salt*
¼ *cup roasted cashews*

In a baking dish, combine all the ingredients, except the cashews, and bake in a preheated 375°F oven for 30 to 35 minutes, covered. Sprinkle the cashews on top and serve.

YIELD: 2 TO 3 SERVINGS

CHAPTER 8

Pasta and Noodles

Capellini with Arugula and Pine Nuts

- 1 *cup sweet tiny red peppers, sliced into flower shapes*
- ¼ *cup plus 3 tablespoons extra virgin olive oil*
- ½ *cup chopped fresh parsley*
- 3 *tablespoons chopped fresh basil*
- 1 *cup pine nuts, ½ ground and ½ whole*
- ½ *cup soy milk*
- 3 *cups torn arugula*
- ½ *teaspoon salt*
- ½ *teaspoon freshly ground black pepper*
- 2 *cups cooked capellini*
- ½ *cup grated Parmesan cheese*

In large saucepan, sauté the peppers in the oil over medium heat for two minutes. Add the parsley, basil, nuts, and milk, and cook for an additional two minutes. Stir in the arugula, salt, and pepper, then toss in the pasta and cheese.

YIELD: 2 SERVINGS

Capellini with Pesto and Shiitake Mushrooms

½ *cup extra virgin olive oil*
4 *cups stemmed and sliced shiitake mushrooms*
2 *cups chopped fresh tomatoes*
1½ *cups Pesto (see page 196)*
1 *teaspoon freshly ground black pepper*
¼ *pound cooked capellini*

In a large saucepan, heat the oil over medium to high heat, then sauté the mushrooms and tomatoes for 7 to 8 minutes. Stir in the Pesto and pepper, and cook for an additional 10 minutes over medium heat, stirring occasionally. Pour the sauce over the cooked pasta and serve.

YIELD: 2 SERVINGS

Angel Hair with Mushrooms and Peas

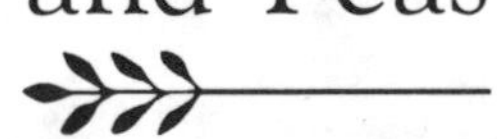

2 *tablespoons extra virgin olive oil*
3½ *cups sliced mushrooms*
1 *cup fresh or frozen peas*
1 *tablespoon salt*

¾ *teaspoon freshly ground black pepper*
½ *cup soy milk*
1 *cup sliced radicchio*
⅔ *cup grated Parmesan cheese*
3 *cups cooked angel hair pasta*

In a large saucepan, heat the oil over medium to high heat and sauté the mushrooms and peas for 5 minutes or until tender. Add the salt, pepper, and milk, cover, and cook another 2 minutes. Add the radicchio and cook 1 minute more. Remove from heat and toss with the cheese and pasta.

YIELD: 2 SERVINGS

Linguini with Garden Vegetables

½ *cup extra virgin olive oil*
3 *tablespoons water*
2 *cups broccoli florets*
4 *cups sliced mushrooms*
1½ *teaspoons salt*
½ *teaspoon freshly ground black pepper*
1 *cup chopped fresh tomatoes*
¼ *cup chopped fresh basil*
3 *to 4 cups cooked linguini or capellini*
¾ *cup grated Parmesan cheese*

In a large saucepan, combine the oil, water, and broccoli, and cook, covered, over medium to high heat for 5 minutes. Add the mushrooms, salt, and pepper, and cook until tender. Remove from the heat and stir in the tomatoes, basil, pasta, and cheese.

YIELD: 2 TO 3 SERVINGS

Spinach Fettucine Alfredo

- 1 *cup sliced mushrooms*
- ½ *teaspoon salt*
- ¼ *teaspoon freshly ground black pepper*
- 2 *tablespoons extra virgin olive oil*
- 1 *cup soy milk*
- ½ *cup Parmesan cheese*
- 1 *cup ricotta cheese*
- 3 *cups cooked spinach fettucine*

In a large saucepan, sauté the mushrooms, salt, and pepper in the oil over medium-high heat for 3 to 5 minutes. Toss in the remaining ingredients, adding the noodles last, combine, and warm through.

YIELD: 2 SERVINGS

Fettucine with a Creamy Asparagus Sauce

- ¾ *cup extra virgin olive oil*
- ¼ *cup chopped onions*
- 3 *cups chopped fresh tomatoes*
- ¼ *cup chopped fresh parsley*
- ¼ *cup sliced green olives*
- ½ *cup soy milk*
- 2 *cups sliced asparagus, bottoms removed*
- 1 *teaspoon salt*
- ½ *teaspoon freshly ground black pepper*
- 6 *cups cooked fettucine*

In a large saucepan, heat the oil over medium heat and sauté the onions and tomatoes for 5 minutes. Add the parsley, olives, milk, asparagus, salt, and pepper, cover, and simmer for another 5 minutes. Toss the sauce with the fettucine and serve.

YIELD: 3 TO 4 SERVINGS

Spaghetti with Eggplant and Garlic

- 1 *medium-size eggplant, peeled and cubed*
- 1/3 *cup extra virgin olive oil*
- 2 *cups diced fresh tomatoes*
- 2 *cups sliced mushrooms*
- 1 *teaspoon salt*
- 1/4 *teaspoon freshly ground black pepper*
- 3 *teaspoons chopped fresh basil*
- 1 *teaspoons dried oregano*
- 2 *cloves garlic, pressed*
- 3 *cups cooked spaghetti*
- 1/2 *cup grated Parmesan cheese*

In a large saucepan, sauté the eggplant in the oil over medium heat for 15 minutes. Add the tomatoes, mushrooms, salt, pepper, basil, and oregano, and cook 5 minutes more. Stir in the garlic and cook another 2 minutes. Toss in the spaghetti and garnish with the Parmesan cheese.

YIELD: 2 TO 3 SERVINGS

Ziti with Fresh Veggies

½ *cup extra virgin olive oil*
¾ *cup sliced carrots*
½ *cup corn (optional)*
1 *cup broccoli florets*
2 *cups chopped fresh tomatoes*
1½ *cups sliced mushrooms*
½ *cup chopped yellow squash*
¼ *cup chopped fresh parsley*
2 *cloves garlic, pressed*
1 *tablespoon chopped fresh basil*
2½ *cups cooked ziti*
¼ *cup Parmesan cheese*

In a large saucepan, sauté all the ingredients, except the ziti and Parmesan cheese, in the oil over medium heat for 10 minutes. Stir in the ziti. Garnish with the cheese.

YIELD: 2 SERVINGS

Ziti alla Pesto con Tomato

- ¾ *cup extra virgin olive oil*
- 2 *tablespoons chopped fresh parsley*
- ¼ *cup well-packed fresh basil leaves*
- ¼ *teaspoon freshly ground black pepper*
- *Dash of salt*
- 5 *cups cooked ziti*
- 2½ *cups chopped fresh tomatoes*

Place the oil, parsley, basil, pepper, and salt in a blender and blend until smooth, about 3 to 4 minutes. Toss with the hot ziti and serve topped with the fresh tomatoes.

YIELD: 2 TO 3 SERVINGS

Farfalle (Bow-ties) with Creamy Tomato Sauce

- 6 *cups chopped fresh tomatoes*
- ¼ *cup chopped fresh basil*
- ½ *teaspoon salt*
- 1 *cup soy milk*
- 2 *cups sliced radicchio*
- 2½ *cups sliced mushrooms*
- ¾ *cup chopped onions*

1 ½ cups sliced asparagus
4 cloves garlic, chopped
½ teaspoon freshly ground black pepper
3 to 5 tablespoons extra virgin olive oil
6 cups cooked bow-tie pasta

Combine all the ingredients, except the last, in a large bowl, toss well, and serve over the hot pasta.

YIELD: 3 TO 4 SERVINGS

Farfalle (Bow-ties)–Garbanzo Bean Casserole

1 ⅛ cups extra virgin olive oil
4 cups chopped fresh tomatoes
1 ½ cups diced green bell peppers
½ cup chopped onions
¼ cup chopped fresh parsley
1 ½ tablespoons chopped fresh basil
1 ½ teaspoons dried or chopped fresh oregano
1 cup canned garbanzo beans
2 cloves garlic, chopped
4 cups cooked bow-tie pasta
1 cup grated Parmesan cheese (optional)
1 ½ cups grated mozzarella cheese (optional)

In large saucepan, heat the oil over medium heat, then cook the tomatoes, peppers, onions, parsley, basil, and oregano, covered, for 25 to 30 minutes. Add the beans and garlic, and cook an additional 5 minutes. Stir in the pasta, then pour the mixture into a large baking dish, and sprinkle the Parmesan and mozzarella on top. Bake, covered, for 15 to 20 minutes in a preheated 325°F oven.

YIELD: 2 TO 3 SERVINGS

Cheese Ravioli with Shiitake Mushroom Sauce

- 2 *tablespoons extra virgin olive oil*
- 4 *cups stemmed and sliced shiitake mushrooms*
- 6 *cups chopped fresh tomatoes*
- 4 *cloves garlic, crushed*
- ½ *teaspoon salt*
- ⅛ *teaspoon freshly ground black pepper*
- 12 *large ravioli, cooked*

In a large saucepan, heat the oil over medium heat and cook the mushrooms, tomatoes, garlic, salt, and pepper, covered, for 10 minutes. Pour the sauce over the hot ravioli and toss.

YIELD: 2 SERVINGS

Leek-Eggplant Lasagna

- 8 *cups sliced eggplant*
- 5 *large eggs, beaten*
- 2 *cups bread crumbs*
- ¾ *cup extra virgin olive oil plus 2 tablespoons for greasing pan*
- 7 *cups chopped fresh tomatoes*
- 1 *cup chopped onions*
- 4 *cups sliced mushrooms*
- 3 *cups sliced leeks*
- ½ *cup chopped fresh basil*
- 2 *tablespoons chopped fresh oregano*
- 1 *teaspoon salt*
- ½ *teaspoon freshly ground black pepper*
- 4 *cups ricotta cheese*
- 1 *cup grated Parmesan cheese*
- ½ *cup chopped fresh parsley*
- ½ *pound cooked lasagna noodles*
- 4 *cups grated mozzarella cheese*

Beat two of the eggs in a medium-size bowl, then dip each eggplant slice in the egg, shake off the excess, then dredge in the bread crumbs. In a large saucepan, fry the slices in ½ cup of the oil over medium-high heat until light brown on both sides. Drain on paper towels. In large saucepan, combine the remaining oil, the tomatoes, onions, mushrooms, leeks, basil, oregano, salt, and pepper, and cook, covered, over medium heat for 20 to 25 minutes, stirring occasionally. In a large bowl, combine the ricotta cheese, the remaining eggs, ¼ cup of the Parmesan cheese, and the parsley. In a large, deep baking dish, lightly cover the bottom and sides with olive oil. Place a thin layer of sauce on the bottom, a layer of noodles, a layer of the cheese mixture, a layer of mozzarella cheese, 1/4 cup of the Parmesan cheese, a layer of eggplant, and then another layer of sauce. Repeat the procedure 2 to 3 more times, ending with a layer of noodles, a layer of sauce, and then mozzarella cheese. Cover with aluminum foil, then bake in a preheated 375°F oven for 30 to 35 minutes.

YIELD: 6 TO 8 SERVINGS

Cold Soba Noodles with Peanut Sauce

- 6 *tablespoons toasted sesame oil*
- 1/2 *cup sliced scallions*
- 1 *cup stemmed and sliced or diced shiitake mushrooms*
- 1 1/2 *cups Spicy Peanut Sauce (see page 197)*
- *Gomasio to taste*
- 1/4 *pound cooked soba noodles*

In a large saucepan, heat the oil over medium to high heat, then sauté the scallions and mushrooms for 8 to 10 minutes. Remove from the heat and stir in the peanut sauce and gomasio. In a large bowl toss the soba noodles with the sauce until all the noodles are covered. Chill for 1 to 2 hours and serve cold.

YIELD: 2 SERVINGS

Japanese Rice Threads

- 1/4 *cup toasted sesame oil*
- 3 1/2 *cups stemmed and sliced shiitake mushrooms*
- 1 *cup sliced scallions*
- 1/2 *teaspoon grated fresh ginger*
- 3 *cups thinly sliced carrot matchsticks, steamed 10 minutes*
- 1 *cup dry rice noodles*
- 1/2 *cup plus 1 tablespoon tamari*
- 4 *cups water*

In a large saucepan, heat the oil over medium-high heat and sauté the mushrooms, scallions, ginger, and carrot sticks for 2 to 3 minutes. Add the noodles, tamari, and water, and cook another 3 to 5 minutes.

YIELD: 2 SERVINGS

Milanese Spaghetti

- 2 *cups chopped fresh tomatoes*
- 1 *cup chopped green beans*
- ½ *cup chopped onions*
- 1½ *cups cubed kucha or butternut squash, steamed 20 minutes*
- 1 *cup cooked corn*
- 1 *teaspoon salt*
- 1 *tablespoon chopped fresh basil*
- ¼ *teaspoon dried oregano*
- ½ *teaspoon sliced garlic*
- 2 *tablespoons extra virgin olive oil*
- 4 *cups cooked spaghetti*

In a large saucepan over medium-high heat, sauté all the ingredients, except the last, in the oil for 10 to 15 minutes. Serve immediately as a sauce over the cooked spaghetti.

YIELD: 2 TO 3 SERVINGS

CHAPTER 9

Main Dishes

Red Potato Casserole

2 *cups chopped fresh tomatoes*
2 *cups peeled, cubed red potatoes*
½ *cup diced red onions*
¼ *cup extra virgin olive oil*
1 *tablespoon chopped fresh basil*
2 *tablespoons finely chopped fresh parsley*
2 *teaspoons dried oregano*
¼ *cup water*
½ *teaspoon paprika*
¾ *teaspoon salt*
½ *teaspoon freshly ground black pepper*
2 *cups diced baked tofu or firm tofu*

Combine all the ingredients in a casserole dish and mix well. Cover and bake in a preheated 425°F oven for 45 minutes.

YIELD: 2 SERVINGS

Tofu Vegetable Crepes

1 *cup sliced zucchini, steamed 5 minutes*
1 *cup sliced mushrooms*
2 *tablespoons safflower oil*
1 *cup cubed baked tofu*
2 *cups Shiitake Mushroom Gravy (see page 191)*
16 *Crepes (see pages 142–143)*

In a large saucepan, sauté the zucchini and mushrooms in the hot oil over medium-high heat. Add the tofu and half the gravy. Mix well, then divide the mixture between the Crepes, roll up, and pour the remaining gravy over them. Serve hot.

YIELD: 16 CREPES

Asparagus with Black Beans and Red Peppers

- *2 tablespoons extra virgin olive oil*
- *1½ cups Black Bean Sauce (see page 198)*
- *12 stalks asparagus, steamed 10 minutes*
- *¼ cup grated Parmesan cheese*
- *¼ cup grated mozzarella cheese*
- *1 cup chopped red bell peppers or fresh tomatoes*
- *3 to 5 stalks chopped fresh parsley*

Oil a medium-size baking dish, covering the sides and bottom evenly. Pour the Black Bean Sauce over the asparagus, then evenly distribute the Parmesan over that, followed by the mozzarella cheese. Bake, uncovered, in a preheated 350°F oven for 15 to 20 minutes or until the cheese melts. Remove from the oven and garnish with the red peppers and parsley. Serve with Peanut Thai Rice Sauté (see page 88).

YIELD: 2 SERVINGS

Chinese Purple Cabbage Rolls with Apples

- 1 *cup chopped shiitake mushrooms*
- 1/4 *cup chopped fresh parsley*
- 1/2 *cup diced carrots*
- 1/2 *cup chopped zucchini*
- 1/4 *cup chopped scallions*
- 2 *teaspoons tamari*
- *Dash of freshly ground black pepper*
- 5 *tablespoons toasted sesame oil*
- 1 *cup cooked wild rice blend or medium-grain rice*
- 1 *cup cooked adzuki beans*
- 1/4 *cup sesame seeds*
- 2 *cups sliced apples*
- 1 *cup apple juice*
- 1/2 *head or 10 leaves purple cabbage, steamed 3 to 4 minutes*
- 1/2 *cup chopped nuts*

In a large saucepan, sauté the mushrooms, parsley, carrots, zucchini, scallions, tamari, and pepper in the sesame oil over medium heat for 5 to 7 minutes. Stir in the rice, beans, and sesame seeds. Set aside. In a separate saucepan, cook the apples and juice over medium heat for 3 to 5 minutes or until tender. Set aside. Place one or two tablespoons of the vegetable stuffing on each cabbage leaf where the thick stem is. Fold the right side of the leaf over it, then the left, and roll up. Place the stuffed leaves in a greased pan and top with the apple mixture and nuts. Cover and bake in a preheated 375°F oven for 25 to 30 minutes.

YIELD: 2 SERVINGS

Sweet Autumn Casserole

- 2 *cups peeled, chunked, butternut squash*
- 2 *cups peeled, chunked, acorn squash*
- 2 *cups peeled, chunked, sweet potatoes*
- 1½ *cups diced turnips*
- 3 *cups unsweetened applesauce*
- 1 *cup pear nectar*
- 2 *teaspoons ground cinnamon*

Combine all the ingredients in a large baking dish, toss, cover, and bake for one hour in a preheated 425°F oven. Serve with brown rice.

YIELD: 2 TO 3 SERVINGS

Spaghetti Squash Italiano

- 1 *spaghetti squash, halved*
- 2 *cups chopped fresh tomatoes*
- 2 *tablespoons chopped green bell peppers*
- 2 *tablespoons extra virgin olive oil*
- ½ *teaspoon salt*
- ¼ *teaspoon freshly ground black pepper*
- 1 *tablespoon dried oregano*
- 1 *tablespoon chopped fresh basil*
- 1 *tablespoon chopped fresh parsley*
- ¼ *cup chopped onions*

Steam the halved squash until done, about 15 minutes. It is done when a strand of spaghetti can be removed easily by scraping the squash with a spoon. Dice the squash and set aside. In a medium-size saucepan combine the remaining ingredients, bring to a simmer, and cook for 10 minutes over medium heat. Toss in the squash, warm, and serve hot.

YIELD: 2 SERVINGS

Potato-Dandelion Cheese Bake

- ¼ *cup extra virgin olive oil*
- 1 *cup sliced mushrooms*
- 1 *cup cubed red potatoes*
- 1 *cup chopped dandelion greens*
- ½ *cup diced baked tofu (optional)*
- 2 *tablespoons chopped fresh parsley*
- 1 *tablespoon chopped fresh rosemary*
- 1 *cup grated Swiss cheese*
- 1 *cup grated cheddar cheese*
- ¼ *cup grated Parmesan cheese*

In a large saucepan, sauté in the oil the mushrooms, potatoes, dandelions, tofu, parsley, and rosemary over medium-high heat for 5 minutes. Lightly grease a large loaf pan or baking dish and pour the vegetable mixture into it. Top with the cheeses, cover with aluminum foil, and bake in a preheated 350°F oven for 35 to 40 minutes.

YIELD: 4 SERVINGS

Holiday Mushroom Loaf

3 *cups bread cubes, just moistened with water*
1 *cup chopped mushrooms*
¼ *cup chopped fresh parsley*
1 *teaspoon chopped fresh sage*
1 *teaspoon chopped fresh rosemary*
1 *teaspoon chopped fresh thyme*
1 *tablespoon extra virgin olive oil*
¼ *teaspoon salt*
1 *teaspoon freshly ground black pepper*
2 *large eggs*
½ *cup chopped onions*

Combine all the ingredients in a large bowl and mix well. Pour into a greased 4-cup loaf pan and bake in a preheated 425°F oven for 15 minutes. Then reduce the heat to 350°F and bake another 15 minutes. Serve warm with Shiitake Mushroom Gravy (see page 191) and steamed vegetables or Sweet Autumn Casserole (see page 134).

YIELD: ONE 4-CUP LOAF

Carrot–Lima Bean Loaf with Mushroom Gravy

1	*cup sliced carrots, steamed 15 minutes*
½	*teaspoon salt*
¼	*teaspoon freshly ground black pepper*
	One 10-ounce package frozen lima beans, steamed 10 minutes
¼	*cup water*

Puree the carrots with the salt and pepper in a food processor or blender until the mixture is smooth but firm. Remove, then puree the lima beans and water to the same consistency. Grease a 4-cup loaf pan with oil. Pour the lima bean mixture in first, then the carrot mixture. Bake for 25 to 35 minutes in a preheated 400°F oven. Serve with Shiitake Mushroom Gravy (see page 191).

YIELD: ONE 4-CUP LOAF

Baked Two-Bean Loaf

- 1 ½ *cups canned chickpeas*
- ½ *cup cooked peas*
- ½ *cup chopped onions*
- 1 *teaspoon ground cumin*
- ⅛ *teaspoon ground cardamom*
- ⅛ *teaspoon ground coriander*
- 1 *teaspoon curry powder*
- ⅛ *teaspoon ground ginger*
- 3 *tablespoons sunflower or canola oil*
- 2 *cups mashed, baked sweet potatoes*
- ½ *cup chopped hazelnuts*
- ⅛ *teaspoon ground cinnamon*
- ⅛ *teaspoon ground nutmeg*

Sauté the chickpeas, peas, onions, cumin, cardamom, coriander, curry powder, and ginger in the oil in a large saucepan over medium heat for 5 minutes. Blend the mixture in a food processor or blender till soft, or mash with a large fork in a medium-size mixing bowl. Combine the sweet potatoes, hazelnuts, cinnamon, and nutmeg in another bowl, mashing with a fork until soft. Place the chickpea mixture in a greased 4-cup loaf pan, spreading it out evenly. Spread the sweet potato mixture over it. Bake in a preheated 350°F oven for 40 minutes, then let cool on counter for one hour. Invert and serve in slices. Excellent with Mughlai's Special Indian Base Sauce (see pages 196–197).

YIELD: ONE 4-CUP LOAF

Seitan Parmesan

Eighteen ½-inch slices seitan
- 3 *medium eggs, beaten*
- 2 *cups fine bread crumbs*
- ½ *cup extra virgin olive oil*
- 3 *cups ricotta cheese*
- ¾ *cup chopped fresh parsley*
- 1¾ *teaspoons salt*
- 1 *teaspoon freshly ground black pepper*
- 3 *cups grated mozzarella cheese*
- 1 *cup grated Parmesan cheese*
- 8 *cups prepared tomato sauce or Greek Tomato Sauce (see page 192)*

Dip the seitan slices into the beaten eggs, then cover each with bread crumbs. Heat the oil in a large saucepan and fry the slices over high heat for 5 minutes or until the bread crumb coating is brown on both sides. Place 6 of the slices into a greased 12-inch by 17-inch pan covered on the bottom with tomato sauce. Mix the ricotta cheese with the parsley, salt, and pepper. Place 1½ cups of the ricotta mixture, 1½ cups of the mozzarella cheese, ½ cup of the Parmesan cheese, and 2 cups of the tomato sauce over the seitan slices. Then add 6 more slices and repeat the procedure. Finish with another seitan layer and 3 more cups of tomato sauce. Cover and bake 45 minutes to 1 hour at 375°F.

YIELD: 6 SERVINGS

Dalsaag

- 1¾ *cups dried red or yellow lentils*
- 3½ *cups water*
- *Two 10-ounce packages frozen chopped spinach*
- 1 *cup soy or regular milk*
- 1 *tablespoon salt*
- 1 *teaspoon curry powder*
- 2 *bay leaves*

In a large saucepan, bring the lentils and water to boil, then reduce the heat to medium-low. Cover and cook until the lentils are done, about 15 to 20 minutes. Add the remaining ingredients and cook another 15 to 20 minutes. Serve with white basmati rice or Mushroom and Pea Biryani (see pages 83–84).

YIELD: 2 TO 4 SERVINGS

Mr. Gupta's Matar Paner

- 1 *cup Mughlai's Special Indian Base Sauce (see pages 196–197)*
- 3/4 *cup fresh or frozen peas*
- 1 *cup cubed Indian Cottage Cheese (recipe follows)*
- 1/4 *cup soy milk*
- 1 *tablespoon saffron threads*
- 4 1/2 *teaspoons prepared tomato sauce*
- 1/4 *teaspoon ground cumin*

Combine all the ingredients in a medium-size saucepan, cover, and cook over medium to low heat for 15 to 20 minutes. Serve with Mushroom and Pea Biryani (see pages 83–84).

YIELD: 2 SERVINGS

Indian Cottage Cheese

- 1 *gallon whole milk*
- 1 *teaspoon white vinegar*

In a large saucepan, bring the milk to a boil, then add the vinegar. Pour the mixture through a cheesecloth and squeeze to remove all liquid. Place on a plate, still wrapped in the cheesecloth. Place a large weight on top and refrigerate for 4 hours before using. It will keep for one week.

YIELD: 1 CUP

Eggplant-stuffed Crepes

- 1 *tablespoon chopped onions*
- 1 *cup diced cooked eggplant*
- 1 *cup chopped fresh tomatoes*
- 1/4 *cup extra virgin olive oil*
- 1 *tablespoon curry powder*
- 1/4 *teaspoon ground cinnamon*
- 1/2 *teaspoon salt*
- 2 *cloves garlic, chopped*
- 6 *Crepes (recipe follows)*

Sauté all the ingredients, except the Crepes, in a large skillet over medium heat for 10 minutes. Divide the mixture evenly between the Crepes, roll up, and serve hot. Top with Greek Tomato Sauce (see page 192).

YIELD: 6 CREPES

Crepes

- 2 *tablespoons barley or whole wheat flour*
- 2 *large eggs*
- 2 *tablespoons soy milk*
- 2 *tablespoons water*
- 2 *tablespoons sunflower oil*

In a small bowl, whisk the flour, eggs, milk, and water until well blended. Heat the oil in a crepe pan over medium heat until hot, then pour in half the batter, tilting the pan till the batter covers the whole pan. Cook for 30 seconds, flip over, then cook for another 30 seconds. Repeat with the remaining batter.

Crepes can be filled with berries, custards, sautéed vegetables, and squash casseroles, and topped with a variety of sauces (see chapter 11).

YIELD: 2 CREPES

Squash-stuffed Crepes with Orange Glaze

- 1 *cup cubed butternut squash, steamed 20 minutes*
- 1 *cup cubed acorn squash, steamed 20 minutes*
- 1 *cup peeled, cubed spaghetti squash, steamed 20 minutes (see note below)*
- ½ *cup raisins, soaked in 1½ cups warm water 20 minutes and drained*
- ½ *cup honey*
- 1 *tablespoon chopped fresh parsley*
- 3 *tablespoons toasted sesame oil*
- ¼ *cup orange juice*
- 9 *Crepes (see recipe above)*
- 3 *tablespoons chopped almonds*

Combine the squashes, raisins, honey, and parsley in a medium-size mixing bowl and toss well. In a small mixing bowl, combine the sesame oil and orange juice, mixing well. Divide the squash mixture between the Crepes, roll up, and drizzle the orange glaze over them. Sprinkle with the chopped almonds and serve.

YIELD: 9 CREPES

Note: The spaghetti squash must be removed from the skin by gently scooping it out with a spoon. It will separate into spaghettilike strands.

Eggless Tofu-Pesto Quiche

- ½ ***package soft tofu (16 oz)***
- 1 ***cup Pesto (see page 196)***
- 1 ***Perfect Pie Crust (see page 226)***
- 1 ***cup sliced mushrooms***
- ¼ ***cup chopped fresh tomatoes (optional)***

Process the tofu and Pesto in a food processor until smooth. Set the pie crust in a pie plate and arrange the mushrooms and tomatoes on the bottom. Pour in the tofu-Pesto mixture. Bake in a preheated 375°F oven for 35 to 40 minutes.

YIELD: ONE 9-INCH QUICHE

Arugula-Pepper Quiche

- 1 *cup sliced mushrooms*
- 2 *tablespoons safflower oil*
- 4 *large eggs*
- 2 *cups soy milk*
- 1 ½ *teaspoons salt*
- ½ *teaspoon freshly ground black pepper*
- 1 *teaspoon dried thyme*
- 2 *tablespoons chopped fresh parsley*
- ¼ *cup arugula*
- ½ *cup chopped red bell peppers*
- 1 ¼ *cups grated cheddar or Swiss cheese*
- 1 *Perfect Pie Crust (see page 226)*

In a large saucepan, sauté the mushrooms in the oil over medium-high heat for 5 minutes. In a large bowl, whisk together the eggs, milk, salt, pepper, thyme, and parsley, then add the arugula, bell peppers, mushrooms, and cheese, and mix well. Pour into the pie crust and bake in a preheated 350°F for 1 hour to 1 hour 15 minutes.

YIELD: ONE 9-INCH QUICHE

Apple–String Bean Tempeh

One 10-ounce package tempeh, sliced ¼-inch thick
- ½ *pound string beans, cut into 1-inch pieces*
- 2 *tablespoons sesame oil*
- 2 *McIntosh apples, seeded, sliced, and steamed 2 minutes*
- 2 *tablespoons ground cinnamon*
- ¼ *cup sliced almonds for garnish*

In a large saucepan, sauté the tempeh and string beans in the oil over medium heat until the tempeh is light brown. Stir in the apples and cinnamon and garnish with the almonds. Serve with brown rice.

YIELD: 5 TO 6 SERVINGS

Tempeh with Arame and Fresh Ginger

- 3 *tablespoons toasted sesame oil*
- 1 *cup cubed tempeh*
- ½ *cup arame, soaked in water*
- ¼ *cup chopped green bell peppers*
- 2 *tablespoons sliced scallions*
- ¼ *teaspoon grated fresh ginger*
- ¼ *teaspoon freshly ground black pepper*
- ¼ *cup gomasio for garnish*

Sauté all the ingredients, except for garnish, in the oil in a large saucepan over medium heat for 10 minutes. Add gomasio and serve hot with brown rice.

YIELD: 2 SERVINGS

Middle Eastern Tempeh Burgers with Fresh Salad in Pita

BURGERS

1½ *cups chopped tempeh*
1 *cup canned chickpeas, mashed into a paste*
2 *tablespoons chopped fresh parsley*
1 *cup tahini (reserve ½ cup for sauce)*
¼ *teaspoon ground cinnamon*
⅛ *teaspoon ground cloves*
½ *teaspoon ground cumin*
¼ *cup sesame seeds*
2 *tablespoons extra virgin olive oil*

SALAD

¼ *cup extra virgin olive oil*
¼ *cup fresh lemon juice*
2 *cups chopped fresh tomatoes*
2 *cups chopped lettuce*

4 *pita breads*

Combine the tempeh burger ingredients, less the oil and ½ cup tahini, in a large bowl and set aside. Whisk the olive oil and lemon juice for the salad together. Toss the tomatoes and lettuce together in a salad bowl, pour over the dressing, and toss again. Mold the tempeh mixture into medium-size burgers (6 to 7) and fry in the oil over medium heat till brown, about 4 to 5 minutes on each side. Place the burgers in a pita with salad and top with tahini.

YIELD: 6 TO 7 BURGERS

Hawaiian Tempeh Kebobs

MARINADE

2 *tablespoons tamari*
½ *cup fresh lemon juice*
1 *teaspoon pressed garlic*
¼ *teaspoon ground allspice*

One 10-ounce package tempeh, cut into 12 cubes
1 *cup cubed pineapple*
1 *cup sliced zucchini*
1 *cup cherry tomatoes*
Tangy Orange Sauce (see pages 201–202)

In a large bowl, combine the marinade ingredients, then add the tempeh, pineapple, zucchini, and tomatoes. Let marinate for 2 hours. Skewer, then broil or grill for 10 minutes. Brush on the sauce and cook an additional 5 minutes.

YIELD: 2 TO 4 SERVINGS

Tempeh with Snow Peas and Green Onions

- 1/4 *cup sesame oil*
- 1 *cup sliced red bell peppers*
- 1 *cup snow peas*
- 1 *cup cubed tempeh*
- 1/4 *cup sliced green onions (scallions)*
- *Dash of soy sauce*
- 1 *teaspoon grated fresh ginger*
- 1/2 *teaspoon ground cinnamon*
- 1/2 *teaspoon ground nutmeg*

Heat the oil in a large saucepan or wok until hot, but not smoking, over high heat. Add the remaining ingredients and stir-fry 5 to 7 minutes. Serve with brown rice or Peanut Thai Rice Sauté (see page 88).

YIELD: 2 SERVINGS

Sweet and Sour Tempeh

1	*cup cubed tempeh*
½	*cup chopped peanuts*
1	*teaspoon crushed garlic*
½	*cup cubed pineapple*
2	*tablespoons sliced scallions*
3	*tablespoons tamari*
1	*cup broccoli florets*
2	*tablespoons hot sesame oil*

Sauté all the ingredients in the oil in a large saucepan over medium heat for 5 to 10 minutes, stirring constantly. Serve with brown rice or Oriental Amaranth with Purple Cabbage (see pages 90–91).

YIELD: 2 SERVINGS

Coconut Chickpea Burgers

½	*cup canned chickpeas*
2	*tablespoons tahini*
2	*tablespoons chopped fresh parsley*
½	*teaspoon salt*
¼	*teaspoon freshly ground black pepper*
¼	*cup sesame seeds*
½	*teaspoon curry powder*
½	*cup shredded unsweetened coconut*

Combine the chickpeas, tahini, parsley, salt, pepper, sesame seeds, and curry powder in a food processor or blender until a smooth dough is obtained. Roll the mixture into 3 balls, then press into patties. Dip the patties into the coconut, then place on a greased cookie sheet and bake for 25 to 30 minutes in a preheated 350°F oven.

YIELD: 3 BURGERS

Baked Avocados with Curried Nut-and-Raisin Stuffing

- ½ *cup chopped onions*
- 3 *to 4 tablespoons extra virgin olive oil*
- 2 *cups cooked barley*
- ¼ *cup raisins*
- ¼ *cup chopped cashews*
- 1 *tablespoon curry powder*
- 3 *tablespoons sliced black olives*
- ¼ *cup sesame seeds*
- 6 *large ripe avocados, skinned, destoned and sliced lengthwise*
- 1 *cup grated cheddar cheese*

In a large saucepan, sauté the onions in the oil over medium-high heat for 5 minutes. Add the remaining ingredients, except the avocados and cheese, and stir well until warm. Put sautéed ingredients in a greased baking dish and place avocados over the mixture. Top with the cheese. Serve with Tomato Salsa (see page 193). Bake in a preheated 325°F oven for 20 minutes or until the cheese melts.

YIELD: 4 SERVINGS

Burmese Veggies with Hot Peppers

- 3 *tablespoons sunflower oil*
- 1 ½ *cups sliced red bell peppers*
- ½ *cup sliced green bell peppers*
- 1 ½ *cups snow peas*
- 1 ½ *cups sliced bok choy*
- 2 *tablespoons sliced baby leeks*
- 1 *cup thinly sliced carrots*
- 1 *clove garlic, sliced*
- ⅛ *teaspoon chopped fresh red chilies (see note page 199)*
- 3 *to 4 teaspoons tamari*

In a large saucepan or wok, heat the oil over high heat until hot but not smoking. Toss in the vegetables and seasonings and stir-fry for 1 to 2 minutes, stirring 3 to 4 times; the vegetables should be crunchy. Remove from the heat and serve with brown rice or Oriental Amaranth with Purple Cabbage (see pages 90–91).

YIELD: 2 SERVINGS

Spicy Tofu–Bell Pepper Supreme

- 2 *tablespoons extra virgin olive oil*
- 1 ½ *cups mixed diced green and red bell peppers*
- ¾ *cup cubed yellow onions*
- 1 ¼ *cups prepared mild tomato salsa*
- ¾ *cup canned crushed tomatoes*
- ½ *cup pitted black olives, drained*
- 1 ½ *cups canned garbanzo beans, drained*
- 1 *cup cubed baked tofu*
- ⅛ *teaspoon salt*
- ⅛ *teaspoon freshly ground black pepper*

Combine the oil, peppers, and onion in a saucepan and cook over high heat for 5 to 8 minutes. Reduce the heat and add the remaining ingredients. Cook over medium heat for 10 minutes. Serve hot with Fresh Corn Salad (page 62) or brown rice.

YIELD: 2 SERVINGS

Sicilian String Beans

- 6 *cups sliced mushrooms*
- 3 *cups string beans, strings removed*
- 3/4 *cup chopped or sliced onions*
- 4 *cloves garlic, sliced*
- 1/4 *teaspoon chopped fresh basil*
- 3 *tablespoons chopped fresh parsley*
- 1 *teaspoon chopped fresh oregano*
- 1/4 *cup extra virgin olive oil*
- 3 *cups chopped fresh tomatoes*
- 1 *cup grated Parmesan cheese for garnish*

In a large saucepan, sauté the mushrooms, string beans, onions, garlic, basil, parsley, and oregano in the oil over medium-high heat for 5 minutes. Add the tomatoes, and cook another 20 minutes. Garnish with the cheese. Serve with brown rice or Tomato Rice with Black Beans (see page 94).

YIELD: 4 TO 5 CUPS

Vegetarian Hungarian Goulash

- 1 *cup peeled, sliced potatoes*
- 1 *cup chopped onions*
- 2 *large cloves garlic, pressed*
- 1¼ *teaspoons paprika*
- ½ *teaspoon caraway seeds*
- 1 *vegetable bouillon cube (Morga)*
- 2 *tablespoons water*
- 1 *cup fresh or frozen peas*
- ½ *teaspoon freshly ground black pepper*
- 2 *cups chopped fresh tomatoes*
- 3½ *teaspoons dried marjoram*
- ¼ *cup safflower oil*
- 3 *cups cooked egg noodles*

In a large saucepan, combine all the ingredients, except the noodles. Cook over medium heat, covered, for 30 to 40 minutes, then serve over hot noodles.

YIELD: 2 SERVINGS

Mughlai's Spicy Kadai Vegetables

- 1 *cup cubed Indian Cottage Cheese (see page 141)*
- 2 *tablespoons oil (sunflower, soy, or safflower)*
- 1/4 *cup chopped onions*
- 1/4 *cup sliced green bell peppers*
- 1/4 *cup cauliflower florets*
- 1/4 *cup sliced carrots*
- 1/4 *cup diced potatoes*
- 1/4 *cup whole small okra*
- 1/4 *cup broccoli florets*
- 7 1/2 *cups Mughlai's Special Indian Base Sauce (see pages 196–197)*
- 1/2 *teaspoon salt*
- 1/2 *teaspoon freshly ground black pepper*
- 2 *tablespoons prepared tomato sauce*
- 1 *tablespoon white vinegar*
- 1 *tablespoon Worcestershire sauce*
- 1/2 *cup chopped fresh tomatoes*
- 2 *to 4 tablespoons chopped fresh cilantro*

In a large saucepan, sauté the Indian Cottage Cheese in 1 tablespoon of the oil over medium-high heat until browned. Remove from heat and place in a bowl. Sauté the onions, peppers, cauliflower, carrots, potatoes, okra, and broccoli in the remaining oil in a saucepan for 5 minutes, covered, over medium-high heat. Add the Mughlai's Special Indian Base Sauce and remaining ingredients and cook for an additional 10 minutes, simmering over medium heat. Serve hot with Mushroom and Pea Biryani (see pages 83–84).

YIELD: 2 CUPS

Indonesian Kale

- ½ *cup extra virgin olive oil*
- 1 *cup chopped onions*
- 3 *cups chopped fresh tomatoes*
- 4 *cups fresh or frozen chopped kale*
- 4 *cups diced red potatoes, steamed 15 minutes*
- 4 *cloves garlic, sliced*
- 2 *to 3 tablespoons curry powder, dissolved in 2 tablespoons water*
- ½ *teaspoon ground allspice*
- ½ *teaspoon ground ginger*
- ½ *teaspoon paprika*
- 2 *teaspoons salt*

In a large saucepan, sauté the onions, and tomatoes in oil over medium heat for 15 minutes. Add remaining ingredients and cook an additional 5 minutes.

YIELD: 4 SERVINGS

Okra Curry

- 3 *cups chopped fresh tomatoes*
- 1½ *cups fresh or frozen whole okra*
- ⅔ *cup chopped red onions*
- ¼ *cup plus 1 tablespoon extra virgin olive oil*
- 1½ *cups black-eyed peas*
- 2 *tablespoons curry powder*
- ½ *teaspoon finely chopped fresh coriander*
- 1 *teaspoon salt*
- ½ *teaspoon freshly ground black pepper*
- 2 *bay leaves*
- 1 *tablespoon sliced garlic*

In large saucepan, cook the tomatoes, okra, onions, oil, and peas for 20 to 25 minutes over medium heat. Add the remaining ingredients and cook, covered, an additional 15 minutes. Serve with Mushroom and Pea Biryani (see pages 83–84) or Mrs. Kartalyan's Rice Pilaf (see page 81).

YIELD: 2 SERVINGS

Spicy Okra with Basmati Rice and Black Beans

½ *cup chopped onions*
2 *cups chopped fresh tomatoes*
1 *teaspoon hot sesame oil*
1 *cup sliced okra*
1 *teaspoon chopped garlic*
¼ *teaspoon salt*
¼ *teaspoon freshly ground black pepper*
½ *vegetable bouillon cube (Morga)*
2 *cups cooked white basmati rice*
1 *cup canned black beans*

In a medium-sized saucepan, sauté the onions and tomatoes in the oil for 5 minutes. Add the okra, garlic, salt, pepper, and bouillon cube. Cook for 15 to 20 minutes. Serve hot over the rice and beans, or with Mrs. Kartalyan's Rice Pilaf (see page 81), or brown rice.

YIELD: 2 SERVINGS

Macrobiotic Platter with Tahini Oat Sauce

¼ *cup toasted sesame oil*
½ *cup chopped onions*
¼ *cup chopped acorn squash, steamed 20 minutes*
¼ *cup chopped turnips, steamed 15 minutes*
¼ *cup sliced carrots, steamed 15 minutes*
¼ *cup chopped parsnips, steamed 15 minutes*
2 *to 4 tablespoons tamari (depending on desired saltiness)*
¼ *cup sesame seeds*
1 *cup cooked short-grain brown rice*
1 *cup cooked or canned adzuki beans*
1 *cup Japanese Hijiki (see page 99)*
3 *tablespoons gomasio to garnish*
1 *cup Tahini Oat Sauce (see pages 198–199)*

Heat the oil over medium heat in a large saucepan, then sauté the onions, squash, turnips, carrots, parsnips, tamari, and sesame seeds for 5 minutes. Place on a plate with the brown rice, adzuki beans, and hijiki. Serve with gomasio and Tahini Oat Sauce on the side.

YIELD: 2 SERVINGS

Hot and Spicy Baked Tofu and Broccoli Stir-Fry

- 2 *tablespoons hot sesame oil*
- 1 *cup cubed baked tofu*
- 2 *cups broccoli florets*
- 1 *teaspoon cornstarch, dissolved in ½ cup water at room temperature*
- 2 *tablespoons tamari*
- ¼ *teaspoon hot red pepper flakes (optional)*
- 1 *teaspoon grated fresh ginger*
- 2 *cloves garlic, minced*

In a medium-size saucepan, sauté the tofu and broccoli in oil for 3 minutes over medium heat. Remove from the pan and place the mixture in a bowl. Combine the remaining ingredients in the pan. Cook on medium-low heat until simmering for one minute. Add the broccoli mixture and cook, covered, for 2 minutes. Stir well and serve with short-grain brown rice or Far East Rice Noodles (see page 166).

YIELD: 2 TO 3 SERVINGS

Moroccan Couscous Sauté

- 1/4 *cup sliced carrots*
- 1/4 *cup diced parsnips, steamed 15 minutes*
- 2 *to 3 tablespoons sesame oil*
- 1/2 *cup arame, soaked according to instructions on package*
- 2 *cups cooked couscous*
- 2 *tablespoons chopped fresh cilantro*
- 3 *to 4 tablespoons tamari*
- 1/4 *cup sesame seeds*

Sauté the carrots and parsnips in the oil in a large saucepan for 5 minutes. Add the remaining ingredients and heat for 10 minutes. Serve immediately.

YIELD: 2 SERVINGS

Purple Cabbage and Spaghetti Squash Stir-fry

- 1/4 *cup toasted sesame oil*
- 2 *cups broccoli pieces*
- 2 *cups sliced purple cabbage*
- 1/4 *cup sliced scallions*

- 2 *cups diced cooked spaghetti squash*
- 3 *cloves garlic, sliced*
- 1½ *cups cubed firm tofu*
- 1 *tablespoon tamari*
- 1 *teaspoon salt*
- ¼ *cup sesame seeds for garnish*

Heat the oil till hot, but not smoking, in a large saucepan or wok over high heat. Add the broccoli, cabbage, and scallions and stir-fry for 5 minutes. Add the remaining ingredients, except the sesame seeds, and cook an additional 5 to 7 minutes. Garnish with the sesame seeds.

YIELD: 3 SERVINGS

Bok Choy with Crushed Garlic and Kombu

- ¾ *cup snow peas*
- ½ *cup sliced yellow bell peppers*
- 1½ *cups chopped bok choy*
- 2 *to 3 cloves garlic, crushed*
- 2 *tablespoons sesame oil*
- ¾ *cup cubed firm tofu*
- 2 *to 3 tablespoons tamari*
- 1 *cup kombu, soaked and drained (see note below)*

In a large saucepan, sauté the snow peas, peppers, bok choy, and garlic in the sesame oil over medium heat for 15 minutes. Add the tofu and cook an additional 2 to 3 minutes. Add the tamari and kombu, mix in lightly, and serve with brown rice or Oriental Amaranth with Purple Cabbage (see pages 90–91).

YIELD: 2 SERVINGS

Note: Kombu leaves will disintegrate if stirred vigorously. Soak for 10–20 seconds, drain and use.

Red Potatoes and Green Peas from Nepal

- ¼ *cup diced firm tofu or Indian Cottage Cheese (see page 141)*
- 1½ *teaspoons extra virgin olive oil*
- ½ *cup fresh or frozen green peas*
- ½ *cup chopped red potatoes*
- ½ *to 1 teaspoon turmeric, dissolved in 1 teaspoon water*
- 1 *teaspoon chopped fresh cilantro*
- ¼ *teaspoon salt*
- *Dash of freshly ground black pepper*
- 1 *small white or yellow onion, chopped*
- ¾ *cup water*
- 1 *teaspoon curry powder, dissolved in 1 teaspoon water*

In a large saucepan, sauté the tofu over medium-high heat for 7 minutes in half of the oil, then transfer to a bowl. Add the peas and potatoes to the saucepan and sauté in the remaining oil over medium-high heat for 5 minutes. Add the remaining ingredients and simmer for 5 minutes over medium heat. Serve with rice.

YIELD: 2 SERVINGS

Sautéed Arame with Far Eastern Flavors

- ½ *cup sliced carrots*
- ½ *cup broccoli florets, steamed 5 minutes*
- ¼ *cup toasted sesame oil*
- ½ *cup sliced red bell peppers*
- 2 *tablespoons chopped scallions*
- 2 *to 3 tablespoons tamari*
- ½ *teaspoon salt*
- 1 *cup arame, soaked in 3 to 4 cups warm water and drained*
- 3 *tablespoons sesame seeds for garnishing*

In a large saucepan, sauté the carrots and broccoli in the oil over medium heat for 3 to 5 minutes. Add the peppers, scallions, tamari, and salt, and cook an additional 2 to 3 minutes. Add the arame and sauté an additional 2 to 3 minutes. Garnish with the sesame seeds. Serve with brown rice or Oriental Amaranth with Purple Cabbage (see pages 90–91).

YIELD: 2 SERVINGS

Far East Rice Noodles

- 8 *ounces of dried rice noodles*
- 1/4 *cup toasted sesame oil*
- 1 1/2 *cups cubed red bell peppers*
- 1/2 *cup finely chopped scallions*
- 1 *cup cubed baked tofu*
- 1 1/2 *cups mung bean sprouts, drained*
- 1 *tablespoon finely chopped fresh parsley*
- 1 *tablespoon finely chopped fresh coriander*
- 1/2 *teaspoon freshly ground black pepper*
- 1 *teaspoon salt*
- 1 *teaspoon soy sauce*
- 8 *saffron threads, dissolved in 2 tablespoons water*

In a medium-size saucepan, place the noodles into 8 cups of boiling water for 1 minute. Be sure to separate them as they cook to avoid sticking, and do not overcook. In a separate saucepan or very large skillet, sauté the peppers, scallions, tofu, and sprouts in the oil for 4 to 5 minutes. Toss in the remaining ingredients and cook, covered, for an additional 4 to 5 minutes.

YIELD: 2 TO 3 SERVINGS

Green Cabbage Stuffed with Vegetables and Fresh Herbs

- 1 *cup chopped mushrooms*
- 2 *tablespoons chopped fresh parsley*
- ½ *cup diced red bell peppers*
- ½ *cup diced asparagus or broccoli*
- ¼ *cup diced onions*
- 6 *tablespoons Pesto (see page 196)*
- ⅛ *teaspoon salt*
- *Dash of freshly ground black pepper*
- ¼ *cup extra virgin olive oil*
- 1 *cup chopped cooked red potatoes*
- 1 *cup cooked lima or fava beans*
- ½ *cup pine nuts*
- ½ *head or 10 green cabbage leaves, steamed 3 to 4 minutes*
- 2 *cups prepared tomato sauce*
- ¾ *to 1 cup grated mozzarella cheese (optional)*

In a large saucepan, sauté the mushrooms, parsley, peppers, asparagus, onions, Pesto, salt, and pepper in the oil over medium heat for 5 to 7 minutes, stirring occasionally. Remove from the heat and stir in the potatoes, beans, and pine nuts. Place one or two tablespoons of the mixture on each cabbage leaf where the thick stem is. Fold the right side of the leaf over it, then the left, and roll up. Place the stuffed leaves in a greased baking dish and pour the tomato sauce over them. Top with the cheese, cover with aluminum foil, and bake in a preheated 375°F for 30 to 40 minutes.

YIELD: 2 SERVINGS

Swiss Chard with Scallions and Fresh Ginger

- 2 *cups whole mushrooms*
- 3 *tablespoons toasted sesame oil*
- 2½ *cups diced Swiss chard*
- 1 *cup sliced yellow bell peppers*
- 1 *clove garlic, sliced*
- 1½ *tablespoons sliced scallions*
- 1 *teaspoon salt*
- ½ *teaspoon freshly ground black pepper*
- ½ *teaspoon grated fresh ginger*

In a large saucepan, sauté the mushrooms in the oil for 2 minutes over medium-high heat. Add the remaining ingredients and sauté for 5 to 10 minutes over high heat. Serve hot with brown rice or Millet-Coriander Stir-fry (see page 89).

YIELD: 2 TO 3 SERVINGS

Stuffed Bell Peppers with Italian Seasonings

SAUCE (MAKES 4 CUPS)

8 *cups peeled, chopped plum tomatoes*
2 *tablespoons extra virgin olive oil*
1/4 *teaspoon freshly ground black pepper*
2 *tablespoons chopped fresh basil*
5 *cloves garlic, diced or pressed*

STUFFING

3/4 *cup shredded yellow squash*
3/4 *cup diced red bell peppers*
1/4 *cup shredded purple cabbage*
2 *tablespoons chopped fresh Italian parsley*
1/4 *cup chopped fresh parsley*
1 1/2 *cups cooked wild rice blend*
1 *tablespoon chopped fresh basil*
1 *tablespoon prepared mustard*

4 *to 5 large green bell peppers, stemmed and seeded*

In a large saucepan, cook the tomatoes in the oil over medium-high heat for 5 to 10 minutes. Add the remaining sauce ingredients and cook 20 to 25 minutes over medium heat. The sauce should be boiling slightly. Meanwhile, mix the stuffing ingredients together in a large bowl, along with 1 cup of the cooled sauce, then stuff into the cleaned peppers. Place the stuffed peppers in a deep pan with 3 cups of sauce on top. Cover with aluminum foil and bake in a preheated 375°F oven for 1 hour and 15 minutes or until the peppers are tender.

YIELD: 2 SERVINGS

Collard Greens with Red Lentils and Carrots

1 *medium onion, chopped*
1 *cup sliced carrots*
3 *tablespoons extra virgin olive oil*
1 *package frozen collard greens*
1 *cup canned vegetable soup*
2 *cups cooked red lentils*
2 *cups cooked short-grain brown rice*
1 *teaspoon salt*

In a medium-size saucepan, sauté the onions, carrots, in oil for 5 minutes. Add the collard greens and cook, covered, an additional 5 minutes. Stir in the remaining ingredients, mix well, and cook another 5 minutes.

YIELD: 2 SERVINGS

Basil Pizza

- 3 *cups rye flour*
- 1 *tablespoon quick-rising yeast*
- 1 *teaspoon date sugar*
- 2 ½ *teaspoons oil (sunflower, sesame, or extra virgin olive)*
- 2 ¾ *teaspoons water*
- 6 *fresh basil leaves*
- 3 *cups Greek Tomato Sauce (see page 192)*
- 1 ½ *cups shredded mozzarella cheese*

In a large bowl, mix the flour, yeast, and date sugar. Add the oil and water and mix. Knead the dough for 3 minutes, then place in a bowl and let rise, covered with a cloth, till doubled in volume. Roll the dough out to a circle 12 to 14 inches in diameter. Grease the pie pan and let the dough rise again for 10 minutes. Add sauce and toppings, then cook in a preheated 450°F oven for 15 to 20 minutes or until the crust is nicely browned.

YIELD: 1 LARGE PIE

Note: Variations for toppings might include ½ cup broccoli or ½ cup fresh shiitake mushrooms.

Basil Pizza

CHAPTER 10

Fish

Tuna with Sesame-Orange Sauce

- ½ *cup sesame seeds*
- 2 *oranges, peeled, sliced, and seeded*
- 1 *tablespoon toasted sesame oil*
- *Dash of soy sauce*
- 1 *cup orange juice*
- *One 12-ounce tuna steak*

In a large bowl, combine the sesame seeds, oranges, oil, soy sauce, and orange juice, and mix well. Place the tuna steak in the bowl and marinate for 1 hour in the refrigerator. Remove the steak from the marinade and broil about 8 to 10 minutes on each side. Serve with a short-grain brown rice.

YIELD: 1 SERVING

Grilled Tuna with Tomato and Basil

One 8-ounce tuna steak
¼ *cup extra virgin olive oil*
1 *slice thick Italian bread*
¼ *teaspoon salt*
1 *cup chopped fresh tomatoes*
½ *cup chopped fresh basil*

Place the tuna steak in a broiler for 10 minutes on each side. Remove from the heat and cool to room temperature. In a small saucepan, heat the oil over medium-high heat, then sauté both sides of the bread with the salt until browned. Drain on a paper towel. Combine the tuna, tomatoes, and basil in a small bowl and serve over the bread.

YIELD: 1 SERVING

Tangy Lemon Tuna–Vegetable Kebobs

1½ *to 2 fillets fresh tuna, cut into 28 to 30 bite-size pieces (1 pound)*
1 *cup fresh lemon juice*

3 *teaspoons tamari*
2 *cloves garlic, pressed*
1 ½ *cups thickly sliced green bell peppers or zucchini*
1 ½ *cups mushroom caps*
1 ½ *cups cherry tomatoes*
1 ½ *cups large Bermuda onion cubes*
¼ *teaspoon salt*
¼ *teaspoon freshly ground black pepper*

In a medium-size bowl, combine the fish, lemon juice, tamari, and garlic. Cover and let marinate in the refrigerator for ½ to 1 hour. Alternating, place the vegetables and fish on skewers, beginning and ending with a vegetable. Place the kebobs in a preheated broiler over any type of pan or cookie sheet to catch any juice. Baste with the marinade, then sprinkle with half of the salt and pepper. Broil for 5 minutes, then flip the kebobs over, baste again, and sprinkle with the remaining salt and pepper. Broil an additional 5 minutes or till done. Serve with rice.

YIELD: 6 KEBOBS, 2 TO 3 SERVINGS

Note: Swordfish or any meaty fish may be used instead of the tuna.

Broiled Swordfish with a Warm Herb Vinaigrette

Two 8-ounce swordfish steaks
Juice of one lemon
1 *tablespoon finely chopped fresh dill*
2/3 *cup of Fresh Herb Vinaigrette* *(see page 194)*
1 1/2 *cups each baby carrots, zucchini, and snow peas, steamed 15 minutes*

Marinate the swordfish steaks in the lemon juice and dill for 30 minutes. Place the steaks in the broiler for 15 minutes on the first side and 10 minutes on the other side. Warm the vinaigrette, but do not simmer, for 2 minutes over low heat. Serve over steaks with the vegetables on the side and brown rice.

YIELD: 2 SERVINGS

Swordfish with Teriyaki Sauce

3 *cups stemmed and sliced shiitake mushrooms*
1 *cup sliced scallions*
3 *tablespoons tamari*
3 *cloves garlic, crushed*
1/2 *cup kombu (optional)*

3 *tablespoons toasted sesame oil*
Two 8-ounce swordfish steaks
2 *tablespoons sesame seeds*
1 *lemon, cut into wedges*

In a large saucepan, sauté the mushrooms, scallions, tamari, garlic, and kombu in the oil over medium heat for 5 minutes. Broil the fish till done, 10 minutes on each side. Pour the sauce over the fish, garnish with the sesame seeds, and serve with the lemon wedges on the side.

YIELD: 2 TO 3 SERVINGS

Note: You can use any firm-fleshed fish in place of the swordfish. Fish is done when it is no longer pink in the center.

Poached Salmon Tomato Stew

Two 1-pound salmon steaks
4 *cups chopped fresh tomatoes*
1 *cup thickly sliced onions*
3/4 *cup chopped fresh parsley*
1 *teaspoon salt*
1/2 *teaspoon freshly ground black pepper*
1 *bunch (about 2 cups) asparagus, trimmed*
1/2 *cup water*
1 *vegetable bouillon cube (Morga)*
2 *bay leaves*

Combine all the ingredients in a deep baking dish, cover, and bake in a preheated 375°F oven for 25 to 30 minutes or until simmering and fish flakes with a fork.

YIELD: 2 SERVINGS

Broiled Salmon Steaks with Dill

Two 8-ounce salmon steaks
- 4 ***tablespoons (½ stick) butter***
- 1 ***tablespoon chopped fresh dill***
- ⅛ ***teaspoon salt***
- ½ ***lemon, cut into wedges***

Broil the salmon steaks on one side for 10 to 15 minutes. Flip them over, place butter slices on top, and sprinkle with the dill and salt. Broil an additional 10 to 15 minutes until the fish is nicely browned. Serve hot with rice or on a bed of cooked dark greens (spinach or dandelion) and garnish with lemon.

YIELD: 2 SERVINGS

Stewed Halibut with Tomatoes and Herbs

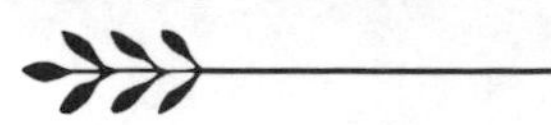

1	*vegetable bouillon cube (Morga)*
½	*cup water*
	Two 1-pound halibut steaks
1	*cup chopped fresh tomatoes*
¼	*cup chopped fresh parsley*
2	*tablespoons chopped onions*
1	*clove garlic*
1½	*teaspoons dried oregano*
½	*teaspoon salt*

In a large saucepan, dissolve the bouillon cube in the water. Lay the steaks in the bouillon and place the remaining ingredients on top. Cook, covered, over medium heat for 15 minutes.

YIELD: 2 SERVINGS

Spicy Sesame Sea Bass with Peppers and Mushrooms

- 5 *tablespoons toasted or hot sesame oil*
- 2 *cups julienned red bell peppers*
- 3 *cups stemmed and sliced shiitake mushrooms*
- 1 *teaspoon grated fresh ginger*
- ¼ *cup tamari*
- 3 *teaspoons sliced garlic*
- *Two 8-ounce sea bass fillets*
- 1 *to 2 tablespoons fresh coriander leaves for garnish*

In a medium-size skillet, sauté the peppers, mushrooms, and ginger, and sauté in 1 tablespoon of the oil for 3 minutes over high heat. Drain off excess liquid and add the tamari, 2 tablespoons of the oil, and the garlic, and cook over medium heat for 1 more minute. In a separate pan, combine the remaining oil and heat on high till hot, add the fillets, cover, and cook for 3 to 4 minutes. Reduce the heat to medium, then turn the fillets over with a spatula and cook, uncovered, for an additional 3 to 5 minutes or until done. Pour the red pepper mixture over the fish and serve garnished with coriander leaves.

YIELD: 2 SERVINGS

Saffron Sea Bass with Tomatoes and Leeks

½ *cup extra virgin olive oil*
3 *cups chopped fresh tomatoes*
1 *cup chopped leeks*
8 *saffron threads, soaked in 1 tablespoon water*
1 *tablespoon chopped fresh coriander*
1 *tablespoon chopped fresh parsley*
¼ *teaspoon salt*
Dash of freshly ground black pepper
Two 8-ounce sea bass or halibut fillets

In a large skillet, combine the oil, tomatoes, leeks, saffron, herbs, salt, and pepper. Sauté for 7 to 10 minutes over high heat. Remove from the heat. Broil sea bass fillets for 8 minutes on each side or until done. Top with the sauce and serve immediately with any type of rice.

YIELD: 2 SERVINGS

Fillet of Sole Oregano

- 2 *tablespoons extra virgin olive oil*
- 2 *medium eggs, beaten*
- 1 *cup fine bread crumbs*
- 1 *cup whole wheat flour*
- 1 *teaspoon minced fresh oregano*
- ¼ *teaspoon salt*
- ⅛ *teaspoon freshly ground black pepper*
- *Two 8-ounce sole fillets*
- 1 *lemon, cut into wedges*

Heat the oil in a large skillet. Place the eggs in a large bowl and the bread crumbs on a large plate. Combine the flour, oregano, salt, and pepper on another plate and mix well. Dip the fish fillets in the egg, coat both sides with the bread crumbs, and then dip in the flour mixture. Fry for 6 to 8 minutes on medium heat allowing 3 to 4 minutes on each side. Serve with a wedge of lemon and a side dish of spaghetti squash.

YIELD: 2 SERVINGS

Fillet of Sole with Fresh Herbs

Two 8-ounce sole fillets
1 *cup (2 sticks) butter*
1 *tablespoon finely chopped fresh parsley*
1 *tablespoon finely chopped fresh dill*
1 *teaspoon finely chopped fresh coriander*
⅛ *teaspoon salt*
Dash of freshly ground black pepper
3 *cups chopped fresh tomatoes*
½ *lemon, cut into wedges*

Broil the fillets for 8 to 10 minutes on one side. In a skillet, melt the butter and add the fresh herbs, salt, and pepper, and cook for 1 to 2 minutes. Pour over the fish and serve hot on top of the chopped tomatoes with the lemon wedges.

YIELD: 2 SERVINGS

Fish Sticks with Tartar Sauce

HEALTHY TARTAR SAUCE

- 5 *tablespoons safflower mayonnaise (available in health food stores) or any type*
- 2 *teaspoons sweet relish*
- 1/4 *teaspoon chopped fresh parsley*
- 1/2 *teaspoon chopped onions*
- 1/4 *teaspoon apple cider vinegar*
- 1/2 *teaspoon fresh lemon juice*

- 5 *tablespoons egg substitute or 2 large beaten eggs*
- 1 *cup water*
- 1/2 *cup flour*
- 1 *teaspoon salt*
- 1 *teaspoon freshly ground black pepper*
- 1/4 *cup extra virgin olive oil*
- 3/4 *cup fine bread crumbs*
- *Three 20- to 24-ounce fillets white-fleshed fish (flounder, sole, haddock), sliced into "sticks"*
- *Lemon wedges*

Combine tartar sauce ingredients in a bowl and mix well. In a medium-size bowl, whisk together the egg substitute and water or eggs. In another bowl, combine the flour, salt, and pepper. Heat the oil in a large saucepan over medium-high heat. Dip the fish into the egg mixture, then the bread crumbs, and finally the flour mixture. Fry for 4 minutes or until light brown on each side. Serve with the tartar sauce and lemon wedges.

YIELD: 12 STICKS

Nori-wrapped Fish Fry

One 8-ounce fillet white-fleshed fish (sole, tile, haddock, codfish, etc.)
1 *large piece nori*
1/4 *cup whole wheat flour*
2 *large beaten eggs or 2 tablespoons egg substitute and 1/4 cup water*
1/2 *teaspoon salt*
1/4 *teaspoon freshly ground black pepper*
Dash of tamari
4 *to 6 tablespoons toasted sesame oil*
1/4 *cup sesame seeds*
3 *tablespoons prepared mustard for dipping*
1/4 *cup tamari for dipping*

Wrap the fish in the nori. In a large bowl, whisk together the water, flour, egg substitute or eggs, salt, pepper, and tamari. Dip the nori-wrapped fish in the batter and fry in the hot oil over medium heat for 5 to 7 minutes or until done. Sprinkle with the sesame seeds and serve with the mustard and tamari.

YIELD: 1 SERVING

Spicy Manhattan Fish Chowder

½ cup diced green bell peppers
¼ cup cubed yellow onions
1 teaspoon hot sesame oil
4 cups chopped fresh tomatoes
1 tablespoon finely chopped fresh parsley
¼ teaspoon salt
¼ teaspoon freshly ground black pepper
8 saffron threads, dissolved in ½ cup water
2 cloves garlic, crushed
1 cup water
½ pound scrod or grouper, filleted and cubed

Sauté the peppers and onions in oil in a large saucepan for 4 to 5 minutes on high flame. Add the remaining ingredients, except the fish, and cook over medium heat, covered, for 15 to 20 minutes. Add the fish and cook an additional 15 minutes. Serve hot over brown rice.

YIELD: 2 TO 4 SERVINGS

VARIATION: Two tablespoons curry powder can be substituted for the saffron threads.

CHAPTER 11

Dressings, Sauces, Glazes, and Frostings

Shiitake Mushroom Gravy

1	*tablespoon sesame oil*
1¼	*cups finely chopped shiitake mushrooms*
2	*to 2½ teaspoons agar-agar, dissolved in 1 cup boiling water*
1½	*teaspoons salt*
¾	*teaspoon freshly ground black pepper*

In a small saucepan, brown the onions in sesame oil for 5 minutes. Stir in the mushrooms and cook an additional 3 to 4 minutes over medium heat. The mixture should be dark brown when done. Add the remaining ingredients and cook over medium heat for an additional 3 minutes till gravy thickens. Serve over rice or fish.

YIELD: 1¼ CUPS

Sweet Onion Gravy

¾	*cup sliced yellow onions*
1	*teaspoon safflower oil*
2	*to 2½ teaspoons agar-agar, dissolved in ½ cup boiling water*
1½	*teaspoons salt*
¾	*teaspoon freshly ground black pepper*

In a small saucepan, brown the onions in oil for 5 to 8 minutes over medium heat. Onions should be dark brown when done. Add the remaining ingredients and cook over medium-high heat for 3 minutes till gravy thickens. Serve over rice or fish.

YIELD: 1 CUP

Greek Tomato Sauce

- ½ *cup chopped yellow onions*
- ½ *cup chopped green bell peppers*
- ¼ *cup extra virgin olive oil*
- *One 16-ounce can (2 cups) whole tomatoes*
- 2 *tablespoons finely chopped fresh parsley*
- 2 *tablespoons finely chopped fresh basil*
- ½ *teaspoon salt*
- ¼ *teaspoon freshly ground black pepper*

Sauté the onions and peppers in the oil in a large saucepan for 5 minutes over medium heat. Add the remaining ingredients and cook over medium-low heat for 25 minutes. Serve hot over pasta, vegetables, or Crepes.

YIELD: 3 CUPS

Tomato Salsa

- 1 *cup chopped fresh tomatoes*
- 2 *tablespoons chopped yellow onions*
- 1 *teaspoon chopped fresh basil*
- ½ *teaspoon finely chopped fresh coriander*
- ⅛ *teaspoon freshly ground black pepper*
- 2 *teaspoons chopped green bell pepper*

Mix all of the ingredients in a small mixing bowl and chill for 1 hour.

YIELD: 1¼ CUPS

Lime Vinaigrette

- 1 *cup safflower or soy oil*
- 3 *tablespoons lime juice*
- 1 *teaspoon chopped fresh coriander*
- ⅛ *teaspoon salt*
- ⅛ *teaspoon freshly ground black pepper*
- 2 *teaspoons chopped fresh parsley*

Combine all of the ingredients in a blender and mix well for 1 to 2 minutes. It can be refrigerated for up to three days.

YIELD: 1¼ CUPS

Fresh Herb Vinaigrette

½ *cup extra virgin olive oil*
1 *teaspoon apple cider vinegar*
1 *teaspoon prepared Dijon mustard*
½ *teaspoon dried tarragon*
1 *teaspoon chopped fresh chives*

Run all of the ingredients through a blender, except the chives, for 3 minutes or till well blended. Stir in the chives.

YIELD: ⅔ CUP

Orange Vinaigrette

¾ *cup toasted sesame oil*
¼ *cup safflower or soy oil*
2 *tablespoons orange juice*
2 *tablespoons chopped fresh parsley*
2 *tablespoons soy sauce*

Combine all the ingredients in a blender and blend until creamy, approximately 2 to 3 minutes. It can be refrigerated and served up to three days later.

YIELD: 1¼ CUPS

Tangy Beet Salad Dressing

1 *cup sliced beets, steamed 20 minutes*
⅔ *cup orange juice*
⅓ *cup water*
1 *tablespoon grated orange rind*
2 *tablespoons balsamic vinegar*

Blend all the ingredients in a blender or food processor, then chill 20 to 30 minutes before using.

YIELD: ABOUT 2½ CUPS

Cranberry Relish

1 *cup dried cranberries, steamed 20 minutes or till they crack open*
½ *cup date sugar*
½ *cup apricot nectar or white grape juice*
1 *teaspoon grated orange rind*
1 *teaspoon fresh lemon juice*
3 *tablespoons chopped walnuts*
2 *tablespoons pure maple syrup*

In a medium-size mixing bowl, mix the steamed cranberries with the date sugar until thoroughly combined. Add the remaining ingredients and chill for 1 to 3 hours before serving.

YIELD: 2 SERVINGS (1¾ CUPS)

Pesto

1/4 cup chopped fresh parsley
1/4 cup chopped fresh basil
1/4 cup extra virgin olive oil
1/4 cup pine nuts
1/4 teaspoon salt
1/4 teaspoon freshly ground black pepper
1 clove garlic

Combine all the ingredients in a blender or food processor and puree. Great over pasta.

YIELD: 1 CUP

Mughlai's Special Indian Base Sauce

2 1/2 cups chopped fresh tomatoes
1/2 teaspoon salt
3 tablespoons extra virgin olive oil
3 cloves garlic, chopped
1/2 teaspoon chopped fresh ginger
1/4 cup chopped onions
1 teaspoon freshly ground black pepper
1/2 teaspoon ground coriander

½ *teaspoon paprika*
½ *teaspoon ground cumin*
1 *tablespoon ground black cardamom*
3 *cinnamon sticks*
1½ *bay leaves*
5 *green cardamom seeds*

Combine all the ingredients in a medium-size saucepan, bring to a simmer over medium heat, and let simmer for 15 to 20 minutes until the flavors are released. Remove the whole spices before using.

YIELD: 3 CUPS

Spicy Peanut Sauce

1 *tablespoon toasted sesame oil*
1 *clove garlic*
¼ *cup smooth peanut butter*
1 *teaspoon pure maple syrup*
1 *teaspoon fresh lime juice*
⅓ *cup plus 1 tablespoon water*
2 *drops hot chili oil or Tabasco sauce*

Combine all the ingredients in a blender and mix until smooth, 2 to 3 minutes. Serve at room temperature over cooked soba noodles.

YIELD: ⅔ CUP

Black Bean Sauce

- ½ *cup canned black beans*
- 2 *tablespoons soy milk*
- ¼ *cup chopped fresh tomatoes*
- 1 *tablespoon chopped onions*
- 3 *tablespoons extra virgin olive oil*
- ¼ *teaspoon salt*
- ⅛ *teaspoon freshly ground black pepper*
- ½ *teaspoon chopped garlic*
- 1 *bay leaf*
- ⅛ *teaspoon crushed red pepper (optional)*

Combine the beans and milk in a blender and mix for 2 to 3 minutes. Sauté the tomatoes and onions in oil in a saucepan for 5 to 8 minutes. Pour the bean mixture on top of this. Stir in the remaining ingredients and cook, covered, for 10 to 15 minutes. Serve with brown rice and grated cheddar cheese.

YIELD: 1 CUP

Tahini Oat Sauce

- ½ *cup tahini*
- ½ *cup finely ground oats or oat flour*
- 1 *tablespoon tamari*

1 *tablespoon chopped scallions*
1 *tablespoon gomasio*
1 *cup water*

Combine all the ingredients in a medium-size bowl and mix well. Serve at room temperature over brown rice or steamed squash.

YIELD: 2 CUPS

Sweet and Sour Salad Dressing

3/4 *cup toasted sesame oil*
1 *teaspoon minced fresh red chilies (any type will do; see note below)*
2 *tablespoons orange juice*
2 *tablespoons tamari or soy sauce*
1/4 *cup safflower or soy oil*

Combine the above ingredients in a blender and blend for 2 to 3 minutes or till creamy. It can be refrigerated for one to two weeks.

YIELD: 1 1/4 CUPS

Note: Wear gloves (rubber or cotton) when working with red chilies to protect your hands from the irritating oils.

Delightful Vanilla Sauce

1 tablespoon arrowroot or cornstarch
1/3 cup plus 1/4 cup soy milk
1 large egg yolk
3 tablespoons pure maple syrup
1 1/2 teaspoons vanilla extract

Thoroughly dissolve the arrowroot in the milk, then whisk it together with the egg yolk, syrup, and 1 teaspoon of the vanilla in a small saucepan. Cook over medium heat, using a square slanted spatula to constantly stir the bottom so it will not burn, until the sauce begins to thicken, then whisk for 2 minutes. Remove from the heat, stir in the remaining vanilla, and serve warm or cold over berries.

YIELD: 3/4 CUP

Orange-Maple Cream Sauce

1/2 cup soy milk
1 teaspoon orange or lemon extract
1 tablespoon pure maple syrup
1 large egg yolk
1/4 teaspoon ground nutmeg

In a small saucepan, combine all the ingredients and mix well with a whisk. Heat slowly over medium heat till thick, stirring constantly with a spoon to prevent lumping and burning. Serve chilled or warm over bread pudding or any type of sweet bread.

YIELD: ABOUT ¾ CUP

Creamy Pear Sauce

- ½ *pear, steamed 10 minutes*
- 2 *tablespoons soy milk*
- *Dash of almond extract*
- 1 *tablespoon pure maple syrup*
- ¼ *teaspoon ground nutmeg*

Combine all the ingredients in a blender and blend until smooth. Serve over any warm sweet bread (zucchini, ginger, etc.).

YIELD: ¾ CUP

Tangy Orange Sauce

- 2 *oranges, peeled and segmented*
- ½ *cup orange juice*
- 1 *teaspoon ground ginger*
- ¼ *cup pure maple syrup*

Combine all the ingredients in a saucepan and bring to a simmer over medium-high heat. Cook for 1 minute and serve hot. It is best over Rice Dream (see note below), ice cream, and any type of kebob (fish, tempeh).

YIELD: 1 CUP

Note: Rice Dream is a nondairy ice cream made from brown rice that can be purchased at most health food stores.

Persimmon Sauce

- ¼ ***cup peeled, seeded, and sliced persimmon***
- 1 ***tablespoon orange juice***
- 1 ***teaspoon lemon extract***

Combine all the ingredients in a blender or food processor and blend on high for 3 minutes. This is excellent served over fresh berries as a dessert.

YIELD: ¾ CUP

Caramel Sauce

1 ***cup date or maple sugar***
1/4 ***cup water***
2 ***teaspoons almond extract***

In a small saucepan, heat ingredients over low heat until the sugar is dissolved. Serve over puddings, cakes, and other sweets.

YIELD: 1/2 CUP

Maple Glaze

1/2 ***cup apricot preserves***
1/4 ***cup pure maple syrup***
1 ***teaspoon almond or lemon extract***

Combine all the ingredients in a small saucepan and cook over low heat for 5 to 10 minutes or until simmering. Pour over cake or doughnuts. It also makes a wonderful glaze for poultry.

YIELD: 3/4 CUP

Almond Butter Frosting

- 1 *cup almond butter*
- 1 *teaspoon almond extract*
- 1 *tablespoon carob powder*
- 1/3 *cup plus 1/4 cup soy milk*
- 1/4 *cup mashed banana*
- 1/4 *cup pure maple syrup*
- 1 *cup shredded unsweetened coconut (optional)*

Combine the almond butter, extract, carob powder, milk, banana, and syrup in a large bowl and mix until smooth with an electric mixer. Stir in the coconut.

YIELD: 3 CUPS

Carob Frosting

- 1 2/3 *cups carob chips*
- 1/2 *cup soy milk*
- 1/2 *cup pure maple syrup*
- 2 *teaspoons vanilla extract*

Blend the carob chips in a food processer till coarse. Melt the chips in the milk on medium heat for 8 to 10 minutes or till fully melted. Add the syrup and vanilla and cook till creamy. Remove from the heat and place on a warm cake.

YIELD: 2 CUPS

Mocha Frosting

¼	*cup rice syrup*
1	*teaspoon almond extract*
⅓	*cup tahini*
1	*teaspoon ground cinnamon*
3	*tablespoons pure maple syrup*
1	*tablespoon Caffix or coffee substitute*
1	*teaspoon carob powder*

In a small saucepan, cook the ingredients over medium heat for 5 minutes, stirring constantly. Let cool before frosting.

YIELD: ½ TO ¾ CUP

CHAPTER 12

Fruit Desserts

Honey-stuffed Apples and Pears

- 2 *apples, cored*
- 2 *pears, cored*
- 1/4 *cup honey*
- 1/4 *cup raisins*
- 1/4 *cup chopped pecans*
- 1 *cup apple juice*
- 2 *cinnamon sticks*

Place the apples and pears in a round baking dish. Combine the honey, raisins, and pecans, and stuff into the cored fruit. Pour the apple juice over them and insert the cinnamon sticks on top. Bake in a preheated 425°F oven for 45 minutes to 1 hour.

YIELD: 4 SERVINGS

Apple-Banana Turnovers

- 1 *banana, sliced and mashed*
- 1 *cup diced apples*
- ¼ *cup maple sugar*
- 1½ *cups oat flour*
- 1 *teaspoon baking powder*
- 2 *teaspoons egg substitute*
- ½ *cup plus 3 tablespoons pure maple syrup*
- 1 *tablespoon ground cinnamon*
- ½ *cup soy milk*

In a medium-size bowl, mix together the banana, apples, and maple sugar, and set the fruit filling aside. In another bowl, combine the flour, baking powder, egg substitute, syrup, cinnamon, and milk in a large bowl and mix well. Roll dough out to ¼ inch thickness with a rolling pin. When rolling make sure flat surface as well as rolling pin is floured with 1–2 tablespoons to prevent sticking. Cut the dough into two equal pieces. Spread fruit filling over the first piece of dough. Very gently, lay the second piece over the filling. Cut out triangles with a knife. Bake on a greased baking sheet in a preheated 375°F oven for 25 to 30 minutes.

YIELD: 6 TURNOVERS

Banana Caramel Custard

- 1 *cup soy milk*
- 3 *large egg yolks*
- 2 *teaspoons vanilla extract*
- ½ *teaspoon almond extract*
- ¼ *cup pure maple syrup*
- ½ *teaspoon ground nutmeg*
- 1 *cup sliced bananas*
- 1 *cup maple sugar*

In a medium-size saucepan over medium-low heat, bring the milk, egg yolks, extracts, syrup, and nutmeg to a simmer. Stir constantly with a whisk and use a tapered spoon to make sure the bottom doesn't burn. Once thickened, remove from the heat and stir in the banana slices. In a small pan over low flame, melt the maple sugar, stirring constantly. Once mixture is dissolved, evenly distribute the sugar between pudding dishes. Pour in the pudding mixture, then chill 2 to 4 hours. To serve, gently loosen the pudding from the sides of the dish by running a butter or small knife around the inside of the glass. Next, place a plate on top of the dish and, keeping them tightly sealed to each other, invert the plate and dish.

YIELD: 2 TO 4 SERVINGS

Carob-coated Nutty Bananas

½ *cup rice syrup*
1 *teaspoon vanilla extract*
1 *cup carob chips*
½ *cup water*
1 *cup chopped unsalted roasted peanuts*
10 *bananas, peeled, frozen, and skewered lengthwise with sticks*

Combine the syrup, vanilla, chips, and water in a medium-size saucepan and cook over medium heat, stirring constantly, until the chips dissolve. Remove from the heat. Roll the frozen bananas in the mixture and then the nuts. Place on wax paper and freeze for one hour.

YIELD: 10 BANANAS

Southern-baked Pumpkin Surprise

½ *cup sliced bananas*
½ *cup peeled, sliced pumpkin*
½ *cup honey*
1 *teaspoon ground cinnamon*
½ *cup almonds, toasted (see note below)*

Combine the bananas and pumpkin in a baking dish. Mix together the honey, cinnamon, and almonds and pour over the fruit. Bake in a preheated 400°F oven for 20 minutes.

YIELD: 2 SERVINGS

Note: Toast almonds by placing them on an ungreased cookie sheet in a 375°F oven and baking for 10 to 15 minutes or till light brown.

Banana Carob Crunch

- 2 *bananas, halved*
- 3/4 *cup oat flour*
- 3 *tablespoons butter or margarine*
- 1/2 *cup pure maple syrup*
- 1 *teaspoon ground cinnamon*
- 1/2 *cup shredded unsweetened coconut*
- 1/4 *cup roasted macadamia nuts*
- 1/2 *cup sugarless carob or cocoa syrup (see note below)*

Place the bananas in a baking dish. In a medium-size bowl, combine the flour, butter, half of the syrup, the cinnamon, coconut, and nuts, mixing in together with your fingers. Spread or crumble the mixture over the bananas. Mix together the remaining syrup and the carob syrup and pour over the bananas.

Bake in a preheated 350°F oven for 25 to 35 minutes. Serve hot or cold with cream or vanilla ice cream.

YIELD: 2 SERVINGS

Note: Sugarless carob and cocoa syrups can be purchased in most health food stores.

Chilled Cantaloupe Stuffed with Cherry Cream

1 cup frozen cherries
1/4 teaspoon lemon extract
2 cups silken tofu
1 cantaloupe, halved, seeded, and chilled

In a blender, combine the cherries, extract, and tofu, and blend for 3 minutes on medium speed until a creamy consistency is reached. Spoon into the cantaloupe halves and serve.

YIELD: 2 SERVINGS

Poached Peaches with Raspberry Sauce

4 *peaches, peeled and halved*
2 *cups apple juice*
1 *teaspoon lemon extract*
2 *cups fresh or frozen raspberries*
3/4 *cup maple sugar*
4 *fresh mint leaves for garnish*

In a large saucepan, bring the peaches, juice, and extract to a boil, reduce the heat to low, and cook for 5 minutes, covered. In a separate saucepan, combine the raspberries and sugar. Bring to a simmer and let cook for 2 minutes. Remove from the heat and serve over the drained peaches. Garnish with the mint leaves. Excellent with vanilla ice cream or Rice Dream (see note below).

YIELD: 2 SERVINGS

Note: Rice Dream is a nondairy ice cream made from brown rice that can be purchased at most health food stores.

Outrageous Macadamia Peach Cobbler

- 5 *large peaches, peeled and sliced*
- *Juice of one lemon*
- 1 *cup apple juice*
- 6 *tablespoons (¾ stick) butter or margarine*
- ¾ *cup honey*
- 1 *tablespoon vanilla extract*
- ½ *cup whole wheat flour*
- ½ *cup rolled oats*
- ½ *cup raisins*
- ½ *cup whole macadamia nuts*
- ⅓ *cup whole almonds*

Combine the peaches, lemon juice, and apple juice in a baking dish and bake, covered, in a preheated 400°F oven for 45 minutes. Meanwhile, cream together the butter, honey, and vanilla in a large bowl. Add the flour, oats, raisins, and nuts, and mix well. Spread on a cookie sheet and bake in a preheated 375°F oven for 15 to 20 minutes or until light brown. Serve the peaches hot or cold with the crunchy topping sprinkled over it.

YIELD: 2 TO 4 SERVINGS

Stewed Plums with Sweet Tofu Creme

- 2 *cups sliced plums*
- 2 *cups apple juice*
- ½ *teaspoon lemon extract*
- ½ *cup maple sugar*
- 2 *teaspoons ground cinnamon*
- 1 *cup Sweet Tofu Creme* *(see page 261)*
- ½ *to ¾ cup chopped almonds*

In a large saucepan, bring the plums, juice, extract, sugar, and cinnamon to a boil. Reduce the heat to low and cook an additional 5 minutes. Let cool, pour into serving dishes, and top with the tofu creme and nuts.

YIELD: 4 SERVINGS

Pear-Hazelnut Crisp

2 *pears, cored and sliced*
4 *plums, peeled, pitted, and sliced*
1 *orange, peeled and pureed*
3/4 *teaspoon grated orange rind*
2 *tablespoons fresh lemon juice*
3/4 *cup white grape juice*
1 *tablespoon orange or lemon extract*

TOPPING

1/2 *cup coarsely chopped hazelnuts*
1/2 *cup coarsely chopped almonds*
1/2 *cup coarsely chopped Brazil nuts*
1/4 *cup safflower or canola oil or melted margarine*
3/4 *cup maple sugar*
1/4 *cup barley or oat flour*
1 *tablespoon ground cinnamon*

Combine the fruit, rind, juices, and extract in a large bowl. Pour into a square 6-inch or 9-inch baking dish. Combine the topping ingredients and sprinkle on top of the fruit mixture. Bake in a preheated 375°F oven for 25 to 35 minutes.

YIELD: 6 SERVINGS

Frozen Banana-Peach Sundae

- 3 *bananas, peeled and frozen*
- 6 *peaches, pitted and frozen*
- ½ *cup fresh blueberries*
- ¾ *cup seedless green grapes*
- ½ *cup pureed frozen strawberries*

Run the bananas and peaches separately through a food processor, until they have the consistency of ice cream, and pour each, one on top of the other, into sundae glasses. Follow with a layer of blueberries and grapes, then top with the pureed strawberries.

YIELD: 4 TO 6 SERVINGS

Assorted Fruit Ices

- 1 *cup water*
- 3 *to 4 tablespoons fresh lime juice*
- 1 *cup sliced papaya, blueberries, pitted cherries, or strawberries*
- 1 *bunch fresh mint leaves for garnish*

Combine all the ingredients, except the mint leaves, in a blender, blend well, then place in an ice cube tray and freeze. Blend the ice cubes in the blender and serve in bowls with a mint garnish.

YIELD: 4 SERVINGS

Mango Pudding Pops

- 1 *cup sliced mango*
- 1/4 *cup soy milk*
- 1/8 *teaspoon ground nutmeg*

Combine all the ingredients in a blender until smooth and pour into pop holders. Freeze 1 to 2 hours.

YIELD: 6 POPS

VARIATION: Substitute sliced bananas for the mango.

Cherry-Coconut Frozen Fruit Pops

- 5 *bananas, peeled*
- 2 *cups peach nectar*
- 1/2 *cup shredded unsweetened coconut*
- 1/2 *teaspoon ground cinnamon*
- 10 *pitted cherries*

Combine all the ingredients in a blender or food processor and blend till smooth. Pour into pop holders and freeze 1 to 2 hours.

YIELD: 12 POPS

Fresh Nectarine Kanten

- ½ *cup chopped nectarine*
- ½ *cup chopped apple*
- 1 *banana, sliced*
- 2 *cups orange juice*
- ½ *teaspoon vanilla extract*
- 1 *teaspoon ground nutmeg*
- 8 *to 10 teaspoons agar-agar*

Puree the nectarine, apple, banana, and juice in a blender until smooth. Bring to a boil in a medium-size saucepan, add the remaining ingredients, and reduce the heat to medium. Cook for 5 minutes, remove from the heat, pour into a mold, and let chill until firm (2 to 3 hours).

YIELD: 2 SERVINGS

Fancy New Zealand Fruit Medley with Saffron Sauce

1 cup chopped passion fruit or juice
1½ cups orange juice
1 teaspoon saffron threads
½ cup halved strawberries
¼ cup sliced mango
¼ cup sliced papaya
¼ cup sliced kiwi fruit
1 cup Rice Dream or vanilla ice cream

Combine the passion fruit, orange juice, and saffron in a medium-size saucepan and bring to a simmer over medium heat. Remove from the heat and toss in the remaining fresh fruit. Serve warm over Rice Dream (see note below) or with ice cream.

YIELD: 2 SERVINGS

Note: Rice Dream is a nondairy ice cream made from brown rice that can be purchased at most health food stores.

CHAPTER 13

Cakes, Pies, and Other Delights

Holiday Gingerbread

- ½ *cup pure maple syrup*
- 2 *tablespoons sunflower oil*
- ½ *cup apple butter*
- 2 *large eggs*
- 1 *teaspoon orange extract*
- ¼ *cup soy milk*
- 1 *teaspoon grated fresh or ground ginger*
- 1 *teaspoon ground cinnamon*
- ¼ *teaspoon ground cloves*
- 1 *teaspoon ground nutmeg*
- 1½ *teaspoons baking powder*
- ¾ *cup barley or oat flour*
- ½ *cup walnuts for garnish*
- 12 *fresh mint leaves for garnish*

In a large bowl, combine the syrup, oil, apple butter, eggs, extract, and milk. Add the remaining ingredients, except garnishes, mixing the spices and baking powder first with the flour. Bake in a greased standard loaf pan in a preheated 325°F oven for 25 to 35 minutes. It is done when the center of the cake springs back when touched or when a toothpick comes out clean. Garnish with walnuts and mint leaves, and serve with Creamy Pear Sauce (see page 201).

YIELD: ONE 4-CUP LOAF

The Perfect Pie Crust

- 2 *cups sifted whole wheat flour*
- 1/8 *teaspoon ground nutmeg*
- *Dash of salt*
- 1/2 *cup (1 stick) plus 1 tablespoon cold butter*
- 1/2 *cup plus 1 tablespoon cold regular or soy milk*
- 1/2 *cup all-purpose flour*

In a medium-size bowl, combine the whole wheat flour, nutmeg, and salt. With a fork or pastry cutter, cut the butter into the flour mixture until it becomes a moist, fine mixture. Add the cold milk by the tablespoon until the dough is of even consistency. Roll the dough into two balls. Flour a smooth surface and a rolling pin with the all-purpose flour. Then roll the dough from the center out until it is 1/2 inch larger than the pie plate. Check by placing the plate on top of the rolled dough. Remove the crust to the pie plate by gently sliding a floured spatula underneath the crust toward its center. Do this around the entire area of the crust, then fold it over on itself and slide it into the pie plate. Repeat the procedure with the second ball of dough, using it for a top crust. Bake at 350° for 15 minutes or till light brown when the recipe calls for a baked crust.

YIELD: ONE DOUBLE 9-INCH CRUST

Pumpkin Pie

- 2 *cups peeled, sliced pumpkin, steamed 20 minutes*
- ½ *cup honey*
- 1 *teaspoon ground allspice or pumpkin spice*
- 2 *teaspoons ground cinnamon*
- 1 *tablespoon vanilla extract*
- 4 *large eggs*
- ½ *cup soy milk*
- 1 *Perfect Pie Crust (see page 226)*

In a food processor or blender, blend the pumpkin, honey, spices, vanilla, eggs, and milk until smooth. Pour the filling into the pie shell and bake in a preheated 350°F oven for 25 minutes.

YIELD: ONE 9-INCH PIE

Orange-Pecan Carob Pie

- 2 *cups rice syrup*
- ½ *teaspoon grated orange rind*
- ½ *teaspoon orange extract*
- ½ *cup carob chips*
- 1 *Perfect Pie Crust (see page 226)*
- 2½ *cups pecans*

Preheat the oven to 350°F. In a medium-size bowl, combine the syrup, rind, and extract. Mix well. Pour the carob chips into the pie crust and distribute evenly on bottom. Then evenly distribute the pecans in the pie crust. Pour the syrup mixture over the chips and pecans and smooth it out evenly. Bake for 30 minutes and cool for 1 hour. It can be chilled and served with vanilla ice cream.

YIELD: ONE 9-INCH PIE

Sweet Potato Pie

- **3½** ***cups peeled, sliced sweet potatoes, steamed 20 minutes***
- **1½** ***cups Vanilla Egg Custard (see page 252)***
- **½** ***teaspoon ground nutmeg***
- **1** ***teaspoon ground cinnamon***
- **1** ***Perfect Pie Crust (see page 226)***

Combine the sweet potatoes, custard, and spices in a large bowl with an electric mixer until smooth. Pour into the pie crust and bake in a preheated 375°F oven for 20 to 25 minutes.

YIELD: ONE 9-INCH PIE

Lemon Pound Cake

¼ *cup safflower oil*
4 *egg yolks*
½ *cup pure maple syrup*
2 *teaspoons lemon extract*
1 *cup oat flour*
1 *teaspoon baking powder*

Combine the oil, egg yolks, syrup, and extract in a medium-size bowl and whisk together well. Combine the flour and baking powder, add to the mixture, and mix well. Bake in a greased standard loaf pan in a preheated 375°F oven for 25 minutes, then reduce the heat to 325°F and bake another 5 to 7 minutes.

YIELD: ONE 4-CUP LOAF

Lemon-Cherry Cake

½ *cup safflower oil*
½ *cup pure maple syrup*
2 *teaspoons lemon extract*
½ *cup piña colada juice*
1⅔ *cups whole wheat flour*
1 *teaspoon baking powder*
2 *medium eggs*
1 *cup pitted fresh or frozen cherries*

Combine the oil, syrup, extract, and juice in a large bowl and mix well. Combine the flour and baking powder, then mix into the syrup mixture. Stir in the eggs, then the cherries. Bake in a greased standard loaf pan in a preheated 350°F oven for 30 minutes. The cake is done when a toothpick comes out clean after being inserted into the center of the cake.

YIELD: ONE 4-CUP LOAF

Linzertorte

- 1/4 *cup honey*
- 1 *large egg*
- 1 *teaspoon vanilla extract*
- 4 *tablespoons (1/2 stick) butter, softened*
- 1/4 *cup whole wheat flour*
- 1 *cup finely ground hazelnuts*
- 1 1/2 *teaspoons ground cinnamon*
- 1 *teaspoon baking powder*
- 1 *cup apricot or raspberry preserves*

In a medium-size bowl, cream together the honey, egg, vanilla, and butter. Combine the flour, hazelnuts, cinnamon, and baking powder, then add to the honey mixture and mix well. Press the mixture into a greased 9-inch pan and bake in a preheated 350°F oven for 20 minutes, then reduce the heat to 325°F, spread the preserves on top, and bake another 10 minutes.

YIELD: ONE 9-INCH TORTE

Black Forest Cake

5 *cups Sweet Tofu Creme (see page 261)*
1 *teaspoon lemon extract*
1 *Simple Carob Cake (recipe follows)*
2 *cups drained black cherries*
2 *cups shredded unsweetened coconut*
1½ *cups sliced almonds*

In a large bowl, whip the tofu creme and the lemon extract for 1 to 2 minutes with a mixer. Set aside. Slice the cake in half and spread the bottom layer with half the lemon cream and 1 cup of the cherries. Cover with the top layer and spread with the remaining cream and cherries. Sprinkle with the coconut and almonds. Refrigerate 2 hours before serving.

YIELD: ONE 9-INCH CAKE

Simple Carob Cake

2 *large eggs*
⅓ *cup safflower oil*
½ *cup soy milk*
2 *teaspoons vanilla extract*
1 *teaspoon almond extract*
1¼ *cups pure maple syrup*
¼ *cup carob flour*
2 *cups whole wheat flour*
1½ *teaspoons baking powder*

Combine all the ingredients in order in a medium-size bowl with a mixer until blended. Place into a greased 9-inch cake pan and bake in a preheated 375°F oven for 25 minutes or until a cake tester poked into the center comes out clean.

YIELD: ONE 9-INCH CAKE

Greek Ravani (Cake in Syrup)

- 2 *cups pure maple syrup*
- 2 *large eggs*
- ½ *cup (1 stick) butter, softened*
- 2 *teaspoons vanilla extract*
- ¼ *cup plus 2 tablespoons soy milk*
- 1 *cup whole wheat flour*
- 1 *teaspoon baking powder*
- ½ *cup cooked Cream of Wheat*
- ½ *teaspoon orange extract (optional)*

In a medium-size bowl, cream together ½ cup of the syrup, the eggs, butter, vanilla, and milk. Combine the flour and baking powder, then add to the syrup mixture and mix well, then stir in the Cream of Wheat. Bake in a greased round 9-inch pan for 35 to 40 minutes in a preheated 350°F oven. Serve soaked in mixture of the remaining maple syrup and the orange extract. Serve hot or cold. The cake is done when a toothpick comes out clean after being inserted into the center of the cake.

YIELD: ONE 9-INCH CAKE

Super Special Tiramisu

- 2 *teaspoons Caffix or coffee substitute*
- 1 *teaspoon lemon extract*
- ½ *cup water*
- 1 *Lemon Pound Cake (see page 229), sliced*
- 2 *cups Sweet Carob Custard (see page 253)*
- 2 *cups Vanilla Egg Custard (see page 252)*
- 2 *cups Sweet Tofu Creme (see page 261)*
- 1 *tablespoon carob powder*

In a small bowl, mix together the Caffix, extract, and water. Place the pound cake slices in a large bowl and pour the mixture over them, using your hands to mix and moisten all the slices. Let soak 2 to 3 minutes. Layer the slices neatly in the bottom of a trifle or other glass bowl. Spread the carob custard over them, then the vanilla custard, and finally the tofu creme. Dust with the carob powder, then chill for 2 hours.

YIELD: 8 TO 12 SERVINGS

Ambrosia Cake

- 1 *Lemon-Cherry Cake (see pages 229–230)*
- 2 *cups Vanilla Egg Custard (see page 252)*
- 1 *cup fresh or canned (drained) pineapple slices*
- 1 *cup orange segments*
- 2 *cups shredded unsweetened coconut*
- ½ *cup sliced bananas*

Bake the Lemon-Cherry Cake in a 9-inch cake pan and cool. Split the cake into two layers. Place half of the custard on the bottom layer and arrange the pineapple and orange slices on top. Place the other layer on top and cover with the remaining custard. Press the coconut and bananas on top.

YIELD: ONE 9-INCH CAKE

Strawberry Custard Pie

1 ½ cups Vanilla Egg Custard (see page 252)
1 Perfect Pie Crust (see page 226), baked
4 cups halved fresh strawberries

Pour the vanilla custard into the crust and chill for 20 to 25 minutes. When ready to serve, pour the strawberries on top of the custard and serve.

YIELD: ONE 9-INCH PIE

BLUEBERRY CUSTARD PIE: Substitute 3 cups fresh blueberries for the strawberries.

Cranberry Nut Bread

- 2 *large eggs or 3 teaspoons egg substitute*
- ½ *cup soy milk*
- 1 *cup apricot nectar*
- 1 *teaspoon baking powder*
- 2 *cups oat or whole wheat flour*
- ¾ *cup date or maple sugar*
- 2 *teaspoons ground cinnamon or nutmeg*
- ½ *cup chopped nuts of your choice*
- ½ *teaspoon grated orange rind*
- ½ *cup cranberries, steamed 15 minutes*

In a large bowl, combine the eggs, milk, and apricot nectar, and mix well until blended. In a medium-size bowl, combine the baking powder, flour, sugar, and cinnamon, and mix well. Fold the flour mixture into the egg mixture and mix well. Stir in the nuts, orange rind, and cranberries. Bake in a greased standard loaf pan in a preheated 375°F oven for 25 to 30 minutes till done. The bread will be a light golden brown color on the outside when done.

YIELD: ONE 4-CUP LOAF

Sweet Potato Spice Loaf

- ¾ *cup safflower oil*
- 1 *cup apple juice*
- 1¼ *cups mashed steamed sweet potatoes*
- 2 *large eggs*
- 2¼ *cups oat flour*
- 2 *teaspoons ground cinnamon*
- 1 *teaspoon ground nutmeg*
- 1 *teaspoon baking powder*
- 2 *teaspoons vanilla extract*
- 3½ *tablespoons unsulfured molasses*
- 1 *teaspoon lemon or orange extract*
- ½ *cup chopped dates*

Combine all the ingredients in the order in which they are listed with a mixer in a large bowl. Pour the mixture into two greased standard loaf pans and bake in a preheated 350°F oven for 35 to 45 minutes. It is done when an inserted toothpick comes out clean.

YIELD: TWO 4-CUP LOAVES

Almond Butter Cupcakes

- ½ *cup almond butter*
- 2 *teaspoons almond extract*

- ½ *teaspoon vanilla extract*
- 1 *cup pure maple syrup*
- 1 *cup soy milk*
- 2 *large eggs*
- 1 *cup barley or whole wheat flour*
- 1½ *teaspoons baking powder*
- ½ *cup chopped almonds*

In a large bowl, combine the almond butter, extracts, syrup, milk, and eggs, and mix well. Add the remaining ingredients, then pour into paper cupcake liners. Bake in a preheated 325°F oven for 25 to 30 minutes or till done. They will be a light golden brown color when done.

YIELD: 12 CUPCAKES

Almond Shortbread

- 1 *cup (2 sticks) butter, softened*
- 1 *cup clover honey*
- 2 *teaspoons vanilla extract*
- 2 *teaspoons almond extract*
- ½ *cup wheat germ*
- 2½ *cups whole wheat flour*
- ¾ *cup whole almonds, toasted (see note below)*

Cream the butter, honey, and extracts together in a large bowl. Add the wheat germ and flour and mix well with a wooden spoon. Press the mixture into a greased 12-inch by 17-inch sheet cake pan, then press the almonds into the dough. Bake in a preheated 325°F oven for 20 to 25 minutes. Shortbread will be golden in color when done.

YIELD: 18 TO 24 COOKIES

Note: Toast almonds by placing them on an ungreased cookie sheet in a 375°F oven for 10 to 15 minutes or till light brown.

The Almondiest Cookies

½ *cup pineapple juice*
½ *cup almond butter*
1 *teaspoon vanilla extract*
½ *teaspoon almond extract*
1 *teaspoon lemon extract*
3 *cups oat flour*
1 *cup almond meal*
½ *cup shredded unsweetened coconut*

In a large bowl, combine the pineapple juice, almond butter, and extracts, and blend well. Add the flour, almond meal, and coconut. Roll into balls, then press into cookies with your hands. Bake on a greased cookie sheet in a preheated 350°F oven for 25 minutes or until brown.

YIELD: 12 LARGE COOKIES

Raisin Oatmeal Cookies

- 1 *cup (2 sticks) butter, softened*
- 1 *cup pure maple syrup*
- 4½ *teaspoons vanilla extract*
- 1½ *cups all-purpose flour*
- ½ *teaspoon baking powder*
- 2 *cups rolled oats*
- ½ *cup raisins*
- ½ *cup chopped pecans*
- ½ *cup chopped roasted macadamia nuts*

In a medium-size mixing bowl, cream together the butter, syrup, and vanilla. Mix together the flour and baking powder, then add to the butter mixture with the oats and mix well. Stir in the remaining ingredients. Refrigerate the dough for 2 hours. Roll into balls, then press out onto a greased cookie sheet. Bake in a preheated 375°F oven for 25 minutes or until light brown and crusty.

YIELD: 12 COOKIES

Tropical Fruit Cookies

- 1 *teaspoon baking powder*
- 2 *cups oat flour*
- ½ *cup (1 stick) margarine or butter, softened*
- ¼ *cup pure maple syrup*
- ¾ *cup piña colada juice*
- ½ *cup shredded unsweetened coconut*
- ⅔ *cup chopped dates*
- ¼ *cup banana flakes*
- 2 *teaspoons vanilla extract*

Combine all the ingredients in a large bowl, mixing the baking powder first with the oat flour. Chill the dough for 1 to 2 hours. Roll into balls and press into cookies onto a greased cookie sheet. Bake in a preheated 375°F oven for 20 minutes or until light brown.

YIELD: 12 COOKIES

Carob Coconut Cookies

- 1½ *teaspoons vanilla extract*
- ½ *cup pure maple syrup*
- ¼ *cup almond butter*
- ¼ *cup carob or cocoa powder*
- ½ *cup buckwheat flour*

½ *cup oat flour*
½ *teaspoon almond extract*
½ *cup chopped almonds*
½ *cup shredded unsweetened coconut*

Combine all the ingredients, except the almonds and coconut, in the order in which they are listed, in a large bowl. Roll 1 tablespoon of dough into a ball, press some almonds and 1 teaspoon of coconut into it, and shape into a cookie. Bake on a greased cookie sheet for 25 to 30 minutes in a preheated 375°F oven.

YIELD: ABOUT 12 COOKIES

Black-and-White Carob Brownie Bars

½ *cup (1 stick) butter, softened*
½ *cup pure maple syrup*
1 *teaspoon vanilla extract*
⅔ *cup ground almonds*
1 *medium egg*
¾ *cup whole wheat flour*
1 *teaspoon baking powder*
1 *tablespoon ground cinnamon*
2 *cups Carob Frosting (see page 204)*

In a large bowl, combine all the ingredients except the frosting in the order given and pour into a large oblong greased 17″ by 12″ baking pan. Bake in a preheated 350°F oven for 20 minutes. Frost the brownies, still in the pan, and chill 2 to 3 hours. Cut into bars.

YIELD: 12 BARS

Sweet Sesame Tahini Cookies

- 1 ***cup tahini***
- ½ ***cup (1 stick) margarine or butter***
- 1 ***cup honey***
- 1½ ***teaspoons almond extract***
- 4 ***cups all-purpose flour***
- 1 ***teaspoon baking powder***
- 1½ ***cups shredded unsweetened coconut***
- ½ ***cup sesame seeds***

Combine the tahini, margarine, honey, and extract in a large bowl and mix well. Combine the flour and baking powder, then add to the mixture and mix well. Stir in the coconut and sesame seeds. Roll the dough into balls and press flat onto a greased cookie sheet. Bake in a preheated 375°F oven for 25 to 30 minutes till light golden brown.

YIELD: ABOUT 30 LARGE COOKIES

Almond Corn Crispies

½ *cup rice syrup*
1½ *teaspoons almond or lemon extract*
2 *tablespoons sunflower or safflower oil*
¼ *cup almond butter*
2 *cups corn or wheat flakes*
¾ *cup shredded unsweetened coconut*
½ *cup raisins*

In a large saucepan, heat the syrup, extract, oil, and almond butter over medium heat for 2 to 3 minutes, mixing well. Stir in the remaining ingredients, then press into a greased 12-inch by 17-inch baking dish. Cut into bars and serve.

YIELD: 12 BARS

Rice Crispy Bars

2 *tablespoons sunflower or safflower oil*
½ *cup rice syrup*
1½ *teaspoons lemon extract*
¼ *cup peanut butter*
2 *cups puffed or crisped rice*
¾ *cup shredded unsweetened coconut*
½ *cup carob chips*

In a large saucepan, heat the oil, syrup, extract, and peanut butter over medium heat until smooth and liquid. Mix in the remaining ingredients until evenly coated. Press the mixture into a greased 12-inch by 17-inch baking dish, then let sit 20 minutes before cutting into bars.

YIELD: 12 BARS

Dried Fruit Balls

- 1 *cup dried unsulfured apricots*
- ½ *cup dried cherries*
- ¼ *cup prunes*
- 1 *cup honey*
- 1 *teaspoon lemon extract*
- ½ *cup ground almonds*
- ½ *cup toasted shredded coconut*

Combine the fruit in a food processor and chop until sticky and rough. Stir in the honey, extract, and almonds. Form the dough into balls, then roll in the coconut, and chill 2 hours before serving.

YIELD: 12 FRUIT BALLS

Mrs. Lutzon's Special Popcorn

1 *cup rice syrup*
2 *tablespoons pure maple syrup*
1 *teaspoon vanilla extract*
3 *tablespoons margarine or safflower oil*
8 *cups popped corn*
1 *cup whole almonds*

In a small saucepan, heat the syrups, vanilla, and margarine over medium heat until the margarine is melted. Combine immediately with the popped corn and almonds, tossing lightly until evenly coated. Enjoy immediately!

YIELD: 3 TO 4 SERVINGS

Carob-coated Peanut Butter Balls

½ *cup peanut butter*
¼ *cup maple sugar*
¼ *teaspoon lemon extract*
1 *cup Carob Frosting (see page 204)*
¼ *cup chopped unsalted roasted peanuts*

In a small bowl, cream together the peanut butter, sugar, and extract. Roll the mixture into small balls, coat with the Carob Frosting, then roll in the peanuts. Chill 2 hours.

YIELD: ABOUT 12 CANDIES

Mrs. Barsamogullari's Chestnut Candy

- 3 ***cups shelled chestnuts***
- ½ ***teaspoon ground cinnamon***
- 3 ***tablespoons pure maple syrup or honey***

Boil the chestnuts in 12 to 14 cups of water for 1 hour over high heat in a large pot. Cool the shells under cold running water, then peel. Take the cooked nutmeats and combine with the remaining ingredients in a blender or food processor. It should be a chunky consistency. Place by spoonfuls into candy paper tins and refrigerate 1 to 2 hours.

YIELD: 12 CANDIES

Toasted Nut Brittle

- 1 *cup whole almonds*
- ½ *cup rice syrup*
- ½ *cup tahini*
- 1 *teaspoon lemon extract*
- ¾ *cup shredded unsweetened coconut*

Combine all the ingredients in a medium-size bowl. Mix well. Pour onto a greased cookie sheet and bake in a preheated 350°F oven for 15 minutes. Cool, then break apart.

YIELD: 2 CUPS

ALMOND COCONUT BRITTLE: Substitute chopped macadamia nuts for the almonds and almond extract for the lemon.

Cinnamon-Maple–Baked Mochi

- 2 *teaspoons ground cinnamon*
- ½ *cup pure maple syrup*
- 1 *teaspoon vanilla extract*
- 1 *piece mochi*

Mix together the cinnamon, syrup, and vanilla in a small bowl. Place the mochi on a cookie sheet or in a shallow pan and coat or brush with the cinnamon mixture. Bake in a preheated 425°F oven for 7 minutes on each side. The mochi is done when it becomes brown and crispy.

YIELD: 2 SERVINGS

CHAPTER 14

Custards and Puddings

No-Bake Maple-Almond Custard

2	*tablespoons apple juice*
2	*cups silken tofu*
4½	*teaspoons almond extract*
½	*cup pure maple syrup*
½	*cup chopped almonds, toasted (see note below)*

Combine all the ingredients, except the almonds, in the blender or food processor and process until smooth. Chill and top with the almonds.

YIELD: 2 SERVINGS

Note: Toast almonds by placing them on an ungreased cookie sheet in a 375°F oven for 10 to 15 minutes till light brown.

Creamy Banana Custard

1	*egg yolk*
2	*teaspoons vanilla extract*
⅔	*cup soy milk*
2	*tablespoons arrowroot*
½	*cup banana puree*

Combine the egg yolk, vanilla, milk, and arrowroot in a medium-size saucepan and whisk well. Cook over medium-low heat, stirring constantly, until it thickens. Remove from the heat and stir in the banana puree and chill before serving.

YIELD: 2 SERVINGS

Vanilla Egg Custard

- 1 ***tablespoon unbleached white flour or pastry flour***
- 2 ***tablespoons plus 2 teaspoons cornstarch***
- 2½ ***cups milk***
- 1 ***teaspoon vanilla extract***
- 4 ***egg yolks, beaten***
- ¼ ***cup pure maple syrup***

Dissolve the flour and cornstarch in ¼ cup of the milk to prevent lumps in the custard. Pour into the top of a double boiler over simmering water and whisk in the rest of the ingredients, except ½ teaspoon of the vanilla, one at a time. Cook for 20 minutes, stirring constantly with a spatula, until thickened. Then whisk for an additional 1 to 2 minutes, remove from heat, and whisk in the remaining vanilla. Chill 3 hours.

YIELD: 4 SERVINGS (3 CUPS)

Note: If you do not have a double boiler, cook the custard in a saucepan over a low flame, stirring constantly to prevent the bottom from burning.

Sweet Carob Custard

- 1/4 *cup pure maple syrup*
- 2 *egg yolks*
- 1 1/2 *teaspoons vanilla extract*
- 1/4 *cup carob chips*
- 5 *teaspoons arrowroot*
- 1 1/4 *cups soy milk*

Combine the syrup, egg yolks, and 1 teaspoon of the vanilla in a small bowl. In a blender or food processor, grind the carob chips. Combine them in a small saucepan with the arrowroot dissolved in the milk and cook over medium heat until the chips melt. Whisk in the egg mixture and cook another 2 minutes. Remove from the heat, stir in the remaining vanilla, and pour into dishes. Chill 2 to 3 hours before serving.

YIELD: 2 SERVINGS (1 CUP)

Italian Coconut Custard

- 2 *egg yolks*
- 1 *tablespoon coconut milk*
- 2/3 *cup soy milk*
- 2 *tablespoons arrowroot*
- 2 *teaspoons vanilla extract*
- 1/4 *cup shredded unsweetened coconut*

Combine the egg yolks, milks, arrowroot, and vanilla in a medium-size saucepan. Whisk well and cook over low heat, stirring constantly until it thickens. Remove from the heat and stir in the coconut. Chill before serving.

YIELD: 2 SERVINGS

Silken Tahini Custard

One 8-ounce package silken tofu
¼ *cup tahini*
¼ *cup pure maple syrup*
1 *teaspoon almond extract*

Blend all of the ingredients till smooth and chill for 1 to 2 hours.

YIELD: 4 SERVINGS

Banana Coconut Pudding

2 *egg yolks*
1½ *cups soy milk*
1 *teaspoon vanilla extract*
¼ *cup pure maple syrup*

1 *teaspoon ground nutmeg*
½ *cup mashed banana*
¼ *cup shredded unsweetened coconut*

In a medium-size saucepan, combine the egg yolks, milk, vanilla, and maple syrup, and whisk well. Cook over medium-low heat, stirring constantly, until thickened. Remove from the heat and stir in the nutmeg, banana, and coconut. Chill 2 to 3 hours before serving.

YIELD: 2 SERVINGS

Delightful Papaya Mousse

½ *cup sliced avocado*
¾ *cup sliced papaya*
1 *tablespoon fresh lemon juice*
2 *tablespoons orange juice*
½ *teaspoon ground nutmeg*
1 *cup halved strawberries for garnish*
Fresh mint leaves for garnish

Place the avocado, papaya, juices, and nutmeg in a blender or food processor and blend until smooth. Pour into small pudding dishes and chill 2 hours. Serve garnished with the strawberries and mint.

YIELD: 2 SERVINGS

Sweet Coconut Rice Pudding

2½ *cups coconut milk*
¼ *cup chopped mango*
¼ *cup sliced bananas*
2 *tablespoons sweetener (maple syrup, papaya juice)*
2 *teaspoons almond extract*
1½ *cups cooked short-grain brown rice*
¼ *cup sliced fresh lichees (optional)*
¼ *cup sliced almonds, toasted (see note below)*
¼ *cup shredded unsweetened coconut*

In a medium-size saucepan, bring the milk, mango, bananas, sweetener, and extract to a low simmer over medium-low heat. Add the rice and stir continuously for 2 to 3 minutes. Turn off the heat and let cool until warm. Chill in the refrigerator for 1 to 2 hours and serve with the lichees, almonds, and coconut on top.

YIELD: 2 SERVINGS

Note: Toast almonds by placing them on an ungreased cookie sheet in a 375°F oven for 10 to 15 minutes or till light brown.

Blueberry-filled Crepes with Orange Sauce

- 2 *cups deseeded and chopped oranges*
- ¼ *cup pure maple syrup*
- *Dash of ground cinnamon*
- 4 *Crepes (see pages 142–143)*
- 2 *cups Vanilla Egg Custard (see page 252)*
- 2 *cups fresh blueberries*
- ½ *cup slivered almonds*
- 1 *cup Sweet Tofu Creme (see page 261)*
- *Fresh mint leaves for garnish*

In a medium-size saucepan, combine the oranges, syrup, and cinnamon, and bring to a boil. Reduce the heat to low and cook 1 minute. Fill the Crepes with the custard and berries, fold the Crepe sides to the center, and serve with the orange sauce on top. Garnish with the almonds, tofu creme, and mint.

YIELD: 4 CREPES

Pineapple Tapioca Pudding

- 2½ *cups soy milk*
- ½ *cup small tapioca granules*
- 1 *teaspoon vanilla extract*
- 2 *tablespoons pure maple syrup*
- ½ *cup crushed pineapple, drained*

In a medium-size saucepan over low heat, bring the milk, tapioca, vanilla, and syrup to a simmer. Cook 3 to 5 minutes or until thickened. Stir in the pineapple and chill for 2 hours.

YIELD: 2 SERVINGS

No-Bake Sweet Potato Pudding

- ⅓ *cup peeled, sliced sweet potatoes, steamed 20 minutes*
- 2 *cups silken tofu*
- 1½ *teaspoons orange extract*
- ½ *teaspoon ground cardamom*
- 2 *teaspoons ground cinnamon*
- 1 *cup maple sugar*
- ¼ *cup soy milk*
- ¼ *cup raisins*
- ¼ *cup sliced almonds*

Combine all the ingredients, except the raisins and almonds, in a blender or food processor and blend until smooth. Pour into dishes and chill. Top with the raisins and almonds.

YIELD: 2 SERVINGS

Cinnamon and Honey Rice Pudding

2½ cups soy milk
1 cinnamon stick
2 tablespoons ground cinnamon
1 teaspoon honey
1 teaspoon vanilla extract
½ cup white or yellow raisins
1½ cups cooked white basmati rice
1 cup sliced almonds, blanched (see note below)

In a medium-size saucepan, bring the milk, cinnamon (both stick and ground), honey, and vanilla to a slow boil over medium heat. Reduce the heat to low and add the raisins. Cook for 2 minutes, then add the rice and cook for another 2 minutes. Refrigerate for 1 to 2 hours and serve. Top with the almonds.

YIELD: 2 SERVINGS

Note: To blanch almonds, place them in a small saucepan with enough water to cover and bring to a boil. Remove from the heat immediately and drain. The skins should rub off easily.

Sweet and Creamy Indian Kheer

- ½ *cup basmati rice*
- 4 *cups soy or regular milk*
- ¼ *cup sliced almonds, blanched (see note below)*
- ¼ *cup maple sugar*
- ¼ *cup raisins*
- *Pinch of saffron*
- 15 *green cardamom seeds, crushed*

In a large saucepan, bring all the ingredients to a boil, reduce the heat to low, and cook, stirring occasionally, for 45 minutes. Serve hot or cold.

YIELD: 4 SERVINGS

Note: To blanch almonds, place them in a small saucepan with enough water to cover and bring to a boil. Remove from the heat immediately and drain. The skins should rub off easily.

Mrs. Gedikyan's Armenian Christmas Pudding

1	*cup whole wheat kernels, soaked in 4 cups of water overnight and drained*
1/4	*cup pure maple syrup*
1/2	*cup rose water*
5 1/2	*cups water*
1/4	*cup raisins*
1/2	*teaspoon ground cinnamon*

Place the soaked wheat in a colander and wash under cold running water. Place the wheat, syrup, rose water, and water in a large saucepan and bring to a boil. Reduce the heat to low, add the raisins, and cook for 35 to 45 minutes. Chill for 1 to 2 hours, then sprinkle with the cinnamon.

YIELD: 3 TO 4 SERVINGS

Sweet Tofu Creme

	One 8-ounce package silken tofu
1	*teaspoon lemon extract*
1/4	*cup pure maple syrup*

Blend all of the ingredients for 1 minute and serve chilled.

YIELD: 4 SERVINGS

Mr. Gupta's Sweet Carrot Halvah

- 3 *cups shredded carrots*
- ½ *cup (1 stick) butter*
- 2 *to 4 tablespoons cottage cheese*
- 4 *cups regular or soy milk*
- ½ *cup raisins*
- ½ *cup chopped almonds*
- ½ *cup finely chopped pistachio nuts*
- ½ *cup finely chopped cashews*
- ½ *cup finely chopped walnuts*
- ¼ *cup maple sugar*
- 5 *teaspoons ground cardamom*

In a large saucepan, sauté the carrots in the butter until they turn red, approximately 5 to 7 minutes, over medium heat. Stir in the cottage cheese and milk and cook an additional 5 to 10 minutes. Mix together the raisins, nuts, maple sugar, and cardamom, and sprinkle over the carrot mixture. Serve hot or cold.

YIELD: 6 SERVINGS

Sweet Cinnamon Squash Pudding

1/4 cup pear nectar
1 cup silken tofu
1/4 cup peeled, sliced butternut squash, steamed 20 minutes
3/4 cup peeled, sliced sweet potatoes, steamed 20 minutes
2 1/2 tablespoons apple butter
2 tablespoons maple sugar
1 to 2 tablespoons water
1 teaspoon vanilla extract
1 1/2 teaspoons ground cinnamon
1/2 teaspoon ground nutmeg
3 to 4 tablespoons sliced almonds, toasted, for garnish (see note below)

Place the pear nectar and tofu in a blender or food processor and blend till smooth. Repeat the process with the remaining ingredients, except the almonds. Chill for 2 to 3 hours, then garnish with the almonds.

YIELD: 3 TO 4 SERVINGS

Note: Toast almonds by placing them on an ungreased cookie sheet in a 375°F oven for 10 to 15 minutes or till light brown.

A Vegetarian's Vocabulary

Adzuki (or azuki) beans. A small reddish bean, usually used in Japanese or macrobiotic cooking. Reputed to be the easiest to digest.

Agar-agar. A clear, flavorless variety of seaweed sold in flakes or in bars that is used like gelatin.

Almond butter. Raw or roasted almonds ground until the consistency is creamy, like that of peanut butter. Usually available at health food stores.

Almond meal. Raw or roasted almonds ground finely until it resembles a coarse meal.

Amaranth. A high-protein grain native to Central and South America that has more fiber than wheat and rice. The grain was grown for nearly eight thousand years until it virtually disappeared for reasons unknown in the early 1500s. Renewed interest in this tasty grain has revived its cultivation.

Amazake. A beverage consisting of either a blend of almonds and water or a dilution of cultured rice. It is available at health food stores under a variety of brand names and in a variety of flavors, such as chocolate, almond, vanilla, and carob.

Arame. A black seaweed that is mild in flavor and aroma. Arame is usually sold cut in thin strands and is added, reconstituted, to soups, grains, or stews, or served as a cold salad.

Banana flakes. Dried, crumbled strips of sweet bananas. Not to be confused with banana chips, which are fried. Banana flakes are simply dehydrated and "flaked."

Barley. A grain often lower in fiber than other grains, but one of the easiest to digest. Its tough outer hull makes barley almost impossible to cook and is removed in a process called "pearling."

Barley flour. Finely ground barley that can be used in baked goods and pancakes as a substitute for wheat flour. Since barley flour lacks the gluten that helps breads and cakes rise, it is often combined with wheat flour.

Basmati rice. A variety of rice grown in India that has a distinctive nutty flavor.

Black cherry concentrate. A thick, concentrated sweetener made from the juice of black cherries. Excellent for use in hot cereals, drinks, desserts, and any other concoction needing a sweetener.

Black sesame seeds. A variety of sesame seed with black coloring, often used in Chinese cooking.

Bok choy. An Asian variety of cabbage that has broad white stalks with dark green leaves projecting from them. Has a mild sweet flavor and can be eaten raw or enjoyed in soups and stirfries.

Bouillon cubes. A concentrated vegetable cube used as a seasoning. Morga is my cube of choice.

Buckwheat flour. A finely ground flour made from the buckwheat grain.

Buckwheat noodles. This unique-tasting noodle is usually found in Asian groceries and is made with buckwheat flour.

Bulgur. A cracked-wheat cereal made from parboiled, crushed grain. Prepared by following the directions on the package and flavoring with a variety of fresh vegetables and chopped mint leaf.

Caffix. A grain-based beverage used as a coffee substitute.

Carob powder and carob chips. Carob is the seed pod of a Mediterranean evergreen tree. It can be ground into a powder or made into chips that taste like and can be used like chocolate.

Chat masala. A powdered spice available from Indian food stores.

Chinese long bean. A variety of green bean.

Cilantro. Also known as coriander or Chinese parsley. Used in Asian cooking.

Coconut flakes. Coconut that has been dried, flaked, and packaged.

Couscous. Also known as semolina, it is derived from a variety of wheat known as durum.

Cream of brown rice; cream of buckwheat. Fine grain cereals made from whole grains which must be cooked before eating. They can be purchased in health food stores.

Daikon. A variety of large, white Oriental radish.

Date sugar. Dehydrated ground dates.

Dulse. A tasty variety of seaweed harvested from American waters that can be eaten dry without soaking.

Gomasio. A traditional Japanese seasoning composed of lightly toasted and ground sesame seeds and sea salt.

Herbimare. A vegetable seasoning salt.

Hijiki. A variety of seaweed sold in thin strands and used in soups and salads.

Kombu. A variety of seaweed sold in long strips or crumbled, it is available in stores as kelp.

Kucha squash. A variety of winter squash which, when peeled, can be added to soups, stews, casseroles, and sauces.

Kudzu, also ***kuzu.*** A starch used to thicken sauces and puddings. Available from Oriental markets or health food stores.

Lotus root. A variety of the ginseng root.

Mâche. Also known as lamb's lettuce, a particular salad green, which is very popular in Europe.

Millet. A variety of grain high in protein and well tolerated by people allergic to other grains.

Mirin. A rice wine used for seasoning in cooking.

Miso paste. Fermented soybean used as a seasoning mainly in soups.

Mochi. A variety of sweet-tasting rice that, when cooked, can be formed into squares that puff up like bread when baked.

Morga. See bouillon cubes.

Nectar. A concentrated fruit juice usually thick with pulp.

Nori. A variety of seaweed sold in sheets or flaked. Nori is most often used to prepare Japanese sushi dishes.

Nu-trim Protein Powder. A complete protein in powder form that provides 8 essential amino acids and is made from allergy-free vegetable ingredients.

Oat flour. A flour milled from the whole grain.

Organic. Food grown in a natural state without pesticides or herbicides. Farms growing organic foods must be certified as such through testing and evaluation by an organic authority.

Passion fruit. A green, sweet, seeded fruit from Brazil.

Pickled burdock. A long, thin root with white flesh and an edible brown skin that is usually pickled and served in soups and stews.

Pomegranate seeds. The edible seeds of the pomegranate fruit.

Rice dream. A nondairy ice cream product made from brown rice.

Rice noodles. Noodles made from rice flour.

Rice syrup. A sweetener made from cooked rice. Available in Oriental markets or health food stores.

Rose water. A light flavoring available in Oriental, Greek, or Middle Eastern markets.

Rye flour. The finely ground grain.

Seitan. A product made from wheat gluten that can be flavored and used in place of meat.

Silken tofu. A creamy variety of tofu.

Soba noodles. A noodle product made with 40 to 100 percent buckwheat flour.

Soy milk. A nondairy "milk" made from soybean mash.

Spike. A vegetable seasoning salt.

Sprouts. Any seed that has been "sprouted" with water.

Tahini. Sesame seeds that have been ground into a paste.

Tempeh. A fermented soybean product.

Toasted sesame oil. Made from toasted sesame seeds ground into oil.

Wakame. A variety of thin, long green seaweed.

Whole wheat kernels. The unprocessed "heart" of whole wheat.

Index